Colonial Postscript
Diary of a District Officer

Colonial Postscript

Diary of a District Officer, 1935–56

JOHN MORLEY

With portraits by Patricia Morley

The Radcliffe Press
London · New York

Published in 1992 by
The Radcliffe Press
45 Bloomsbury Square
London WC1A 2HY

175 Fifth Avenue
New York
NY 10010

In the United States of America
and Canada distributed by
St Martin's Press
175 Fifth Avenue
New York
NY 10010

Copyright © 1992 by John Morley

All rights reserved. Except for brief quotations in a review, this book, or any part thereof, must not be reproduced in any form without permission in writing from the publishers.

A CIP record for this book is available from the British Library

Library of Congress catalog card number available
A full CIP record is available from the Library of Congress

ISBN 1–85043–526–X

Printed and bound in Great Britain by WBC Limited,
Bridgend, Mid Glamorgan

Contents

List of Portraits	vi
General foreword to the series	vii
Author's preface	xi
1 Aden, 1935–6	1
2 Northern Nigeria – Sokoto, 1937–8	21
3 Northern Nigeria – Sokoto continued, 1937–8	33
4 Northern Nigeria – Sokoto concluded, 1937–8	54
5 Northern Nigeria – Zuru and Yauri, 1938–9	68
6 Northern Nigeria – Lokoja, 1939–40	80
7 Northern Nigeria – Ankpa, 1940–1	86
8 Northern Nigeria – Kano – RWAFF, 1940–1	101
9 Eritrea – Massawa, 1941–2	111
10 Eritrea – Hamasien, 1942–3	134
11 Eritrea – Agordat, 1943–4	147
12 Singapore, 1945–6	161
13 Singapore continued, 1946–8	171
14 Malaya – Ipoh and Kuala Lumpur, 1949–51	180
15 Gold Coast, 1952–6	187
16 Gold Coast concluded, 1952–6	200

List of Portraits
by Patricia Morley

1 A Zabirma from Dosso (Niger)
2 Moman Kalgo from Sokoto (Nigeria)
3 Awuni Frafra from Mamprusi (Gold Coast/Ghana)
4 Tahiru Wenchi from Ashanti (Gold Coast/Ghana)
5 Ahmadu Buzu from Gao (Fr. Sudan/Mali)
6 Kofi Misah II Pankesihene (Gold Coast/Ghana)
7 Salonika (Fr. Togoland/Togo)
8 Beatrice the carpenter's daughter from Accra (Gold Coast/Ghana)

General Foreword to the Series

A whole generation has passed, nearer two in the case of the Indian sub-continent, since Britain's colonial territories in South-East Asia, Africa and the Caribbean, achieved independence. In the Pacific the transfer of power came about a decade later. There was little interest in recording the official or the personal experience of empire either in the inter-war years – viewed by some, perhaps those personally involved, as the apogee of the British empire – or in the immediate aftermath of empire. And in this latter period attitudes were critical, largely condemnatory and even purposively hostile. This is not surprising: such a reaction is usual at the end of a remarkable period of history.

With the passing of time and with longer historical perspective it was possible to see events in a better and more objective light and the trend was gradually reversed. In due course there came about a more sympathetic interest in the colonial period, by those in Britain or in the countries of the former empire who were intrigued to know how colonial government operated – in local, everyday practice, as well as at the level of the Colonial Office and Government House. Also those who had themselves been an integral part of the process wanted to record the experience before, in the nature of things, it was too late. Here was a potentially rich vein of knowledge and personal experience for specialist academic historians as well as the general reader.

Leaving aside the extensive academic analysis of the end of empire, the interest in the colonial period in this country may be said to have been stimulated by creative literature. In the late

General Foreword to the Series

1960s there were novels, films, radio and TV programmes now and again tinged with a touch of nineteenth-century romance and with just a whiff of nostalgia to soften the sharp realism of the colonial encounter. The focus was primarily on India and the post-1947 imagery of the 'Raj': there were outstanding novels by Paul Scott – surely destined to be one of the greatest twentieth-century novelists – J. G. Farrell and John Masters; epic films like *A Passage to India*, and later *Gandhi*, or the charming and moving vignette of *Staying On*, and, for Africa, *Out of Africa* and *Mister Johnson*.

In the second half of the 1970s there emerged a highly successful genre of collective 'colonial' memoirs in the *Tales of . . .* format: Charles Allen's splendid trilogy *Plain Tales from the Raj* (1975), *Tales from the Dark Continent* (1979) and *Tales from the South China Seas* (1983), followed by others such as *Tales of Paradise: Memories of the British in the South Pacific* (1986) and *Tales of Empire: the British in the Middle East* (1989), all good history and good reading.

Throughout the period from India's independence until that of the last crown there had, of course, been those splendid works which embraced both academic history and creative literature: for example, Philip Woodruff's *The Men Who Ruled India: The Founders* (1953) and *The Guardians* (1954); and Jan Morris's *Heaven's Command*, *Pax Britannica* and *Farewell the Trumpets* (1973–8).

Finally as the 1970s gave way to the 1980s, those voices which had remained largely silent since the end of empire, now wanted to be heard. The one-time colonial official, be he district officer, agriculturist, veterinary, medical or forestry officer, policeman or magistrate, and just as often their wives, began to write about their experiences in one of Britain's overseas civil services. They wrote with relish and enthusiasm, with a touch of adventure, and few personal regrets. Above all, perhaps, with the feeling of a practical and useful task well done although some thought that more could have been achieved had independence come about more slowly.

These memoirs often began as little more than a private

General Foreword to the Series

record for the family, children and grandchildren, some of whom had never seen a colonial governor in full fig, shaken hands with an emir or paramount chief, discussed plans with a peasant or local politician, or known at first hand the difference between an *askari* and *alkali*, an *amah* or an *ayah*. Soon the colonial memoir began to establish itself as a literary genre in its own right.

The initiative of the Radcliffe Press in harnessing and promoting this talent, primarily autobiographical but also biographical, promises to be a positive addition to both the historical and literary scenes. Here is a voice from the last Colonial Service generation relating from personal experience the lives and careers involved in the exercise of latterday empire. They were part of what was arguably the most influential and far-reaching event of the second half of the twentieth century, namely the end of empire and the consequent emergence of the independent nations of the Third World. It could perhaps also be argued that this is part of an even greater process – decolonisation 'writ large', a sea-change in world affairs affecting greater and lesser powers into the late twentieth century.

It may well be that by 2066, the centenary of the closing down of the Colonial Office, great-great-grandchildren will find the most telling image of Britain's once huge empire in these memoirs and biographical studies, rather than in the weightier imperial archives at the Public Record Office at Kew or in Rhodes House, Oxford.

A. H. M. KIRK GREENE
Lecturer in the Modern History of Africa, University of Oxford, and formerly of the Colonial Administrative Service, Nigeria.

Author's Preface

I would like to explain how this book came to be written. When my mother died in 1959 it was found she had accumulated a vast store of her children's letters, some dating back thirty years. My own bundle was sent to me, but for a long while remained unopened. At that time I had recently embarked on a new career, was taming a large garden and was surrounded by a young family. So it was not until the mid seventies, by which time recollections of my colonial past were already fading, that I began going through these old letters, constructing from them some sort of narrative.

This was done for my own pleasure, and for whatever interest it might hold for my family. In comparison with the memoirs of former Governors and High Commissioners it seemed too slight for a wider audience. Latterly, however, I have felt that changed circumstances may have made it more acceptable. In the first place, the general concept of what constitutes 'history' has widened in recent years; it is no longer confined to the corridors of power, but is equally concerned to explore life at the grass roots. Secondly, with the passage of time it becomes increasingly clear how unique an experience was that of the old-style colonial civil servant. Thirdly, it is evident that the new nation states, former colonies or protectorates, are hungry for any and every first-hand account of this critical period in their past history. This was brought home to me when I saw how eagerly the Eritrean People's Liberation Front seized upon my description (chapters 9–11) of their country as it had been half a century ago. This is not surprising – what would we,

Author's Preface

too, not give to be privy to the impressions of a Roman sub-prefect, posted to the province of Britannia in the 4th century A.D.?

Let me now introduce the narrator, in the year 1935. He comes from a large family, born in a Northamptonshire vicarage but later transferred to Somerset, whose parents did not preach but both sought to practise the virtues of self-reliance and service to the community. He went to a public school where, on Commemoration Day, Kipling's 'Recessional' was still sung as a reminder of Britain's imperial responsibilities. When this story opens he is aged 21, has obtained a degree at Cambridge in classics and history, and has applied for a post in the Colonial Administrative Service, entry to which depended not on an examination but on a series of interviews. Half-way through this process a charismatic Frenchman, Antonin Besse, founder and sole owner of an extensive commercial empire based on Aden, appeared on the scene. A.B. had already recruited two graduates from St Andrew's University, Drew Reid and Sandy Sloan, and now, without too much difficulty, persuaded me to make a third. My parents and friends and the College authorities were dismayed; the Colonial Office were more understanding and readily agreed to hold over my application until the following year, by which time, they calculated, I would have acquired experience of the world which could be useful to me, and probably to them too. And so it proved, and for this reason I have included an account of my year in Aden, although it did not form part of my colonial service career.

I
Aden, 1935–6

King Edward VII is reported to have made the remark that only during his royal progress through India had he come to appreciate the true meaning of pomp and ceremony. Of these traditions the Peninsular & Orient Steam Navigation Company, in one of whose vessels Drew Reid and I were now embarked, had remained a faithful custodian. Its prestige was enormous, for not only was it the sole carrier of mail between Britain and her eastern dominions but it also transported governors, generals, bishops of far-flung dioceses, heads of great banks and commercial firms with power equal to that of governments and names that, east of Suez, were household words. Its officers formed a hierarchy of their own and were considered the first reserve of the British navy, and its passenger list was a microcosm of colonial and overseas society, high and low. It had even added a new word, descriptive of status, to the English language. Passage warrant holders of superior rank were entitled to accommodation on the cooler side of the ship, away from the noonday sun, on the port side for the outward journey and on the starboard side coming home; in clerical shorthand these were the POSH people. Drew and I travelled second class, in a cabin on the starboard side which we shared with a Cyprus prison officer returning from leave. This put us well down the social scale but we were fortunately unaware of the fact. After dinner, when bidden to drink coffee with A.B. in one of the first class staterooms, we would don our dinner jackets and black ties to do so.

On board all the talk was of the war in Abyssinia, where the

Colonial Postscript

Italians were now advancing. In Messina as we passed through the straits at night they were celebrating with a firework display the capture of Adowa, where an earlier Italian army had been defeated and disgraced; and in Cairo A.B. was whisked away to high level meetings with the chief representative of Shell, to discuss the effect of economic sanctions which the League of Nations was talking of imposing.

Among A.B's many interests was a shipping line, consisting mainly of dhows and lighters but with two ocean-going vessels as well, the larger of which, the *El Haq*, had been ordered up to Suez to meet us. In this we now proceeded down the Red Sea, calling at various ports on the way. The first was Jedda, if port it could be called, access to which lay through a gap in the coral reef half closed by the hulk of a pilgrim ship that had caught fire and been stranded there a number of years previously. Inside the reef there was no safe anchorage, so all the work of loading and unloading had to be completed during the hours of daylight, with the ship coming in at dawn and leaving again before dark. The captain had therefore to guide his ship through the narrow and hidden opening full in face of the fiery orb of the sun coming up over the rim of the desert to the east and, at the end of the day, negotiate the same passage steering into the sun descending into the sea in the west. Either way, it was a hazardous five minutes.

These peculiarities of the port of Jedda meant that speed had to be reduced the day before, so that we should not arrive too early. A.B. had a bright idea – why not stop the ship and have a swim? The captain demurred but was overruled, the engines were stopped, down went the companionway and over the side went the intrepid A.B., followed by Drew and myself, whose immunity to sharks had not, like A.B's, been tested by 35 years experience. We thought a quick dip would prove the point, but our employer was already striking off round the ship, where we felt bound to follow him. While this was going on the captain walked round the deck, loaded revolver in hand, so that if we did not perish in one way we were all too likely to do so in another.

Aden, 1935–6

Jedda in those days was a quiet little town, out of the pilgrim season, as the discoveries of oil in Saudi Arabia and the great wealth they were to bring still lay in the future. Hodeida further down the coast was quieter still and almost derelict, though its beautiful carved doorways and balconies spoke of an opulent past. It was here that A.B. had started business as a young man, with £200 capital and in a rented godown. Since then he had made one fortune and lost most of it, and was now on the way to making a larger one. The firm had a branch in Hodeida, through which it traded in piece goods and bought the world-famous Mocha coffee that grows in the Yemen highlands. This coffee is never drunk on its own in Europe, but is used for blending with others. We assisted in the process, since all the coffee bought in Hodeida was sent to Aden, where we would adulterate it by at least 20 to 30 per cent, using for this purpose some cheap beans from another part of the Arabian coast which were undistinguishable in appearance but had none of the Mocha flavour. This seemed highly immoral but, A.B. assured me, all Mocha coffee was marketed in this state and his was better than any. (Not that one would think so, seeing the complaints that often came from buyers.) Furthermore, he continued with scorn, what was the good of sending quality coffee to Europe now that the main market had moved from Le Havre, where it had been before the war, and where knowledgable Frenchmen judged it on its taste, to London where the English judged coffee by its appearance? So we continued to adulterate the coffee as much as we dared, and I soon became quite adept at doing so.

There was one more port of call before passing Perim and out into the Indian Ocean. This was the small island of Kamaran, which served as the health inspection station for all pilgrims coming by sea from the east. Here there was a British Residency and a British Resident, a Major Thompson who had recently acquired fame in a rather unusual manner. Imperial Airways had begun using Kamaran as a halting place for its aircraft, in the days when rather frequent stops had to be made for refuelling. When the first flight arrived, Major Thompson invited

Colonial Postscript

crew and passengers to breakfast at the Residency. With the next flight he did the same, and so with the next and the next, the captain of the aircraft always assuming that this entertainment had been arranged by the company, the Major merely accepting each set of visitors as strangers entitled to his hospitality. And so, the story went, matters continued for a whole year until the true state of affairs was discovered.

Two nights and a day later the *El Haq* dropped her anchors off Aden. No need to describe here the barren rocks so well known to the millions of travellers who have passed this way, although we were heading not for the trim villas clustering round the Residency at Steamer Point but for the old town which lay out of sight on the other side. A letter home gave my first impression of this and of the House of Besse which, very deliberately, turned its back on the main administrative centre and on European society.

'Crater is separated from Steamer Point by an arm of rock stretching into the sea, which the road crosses by a pass that has been cut through the hill, rather like a section of the Cheddar Gorge,' I wrote.

> Like Steamer Point, Crater is huddled together on the only flat ground between the hills and the sea, and it is this great wall of rock which reflects the midday sun and intensifies it, but shuts off sooner the sun in the evening. The office, and A.B's house, is in one of the town blocks near the hill. The ground floor is occupied by the main office, which is one large and irregularly shaped room, where each of the departments has a corner to itself. Also on the ground floor and much larger in size is the big hide and skin godown, where some of the hides and skins passing through our hands are sorted, weighed and packed for their destinations in Europe. A good many are sorted at the branches and these go straight to Europe without coming to Aden at all, or if they have to come here, they are put in lighters lying in the harbour, so that they can be transhipped as soon as there is a boat available, and avoid paying any landing charges. There are two other

godowns, or stores, one for skins, the other for import goods, like flour or sugar, for beeswax, and for coffee. Most of the coffee is cleaned at the branches, but what is not is done by the native women here. It is done by a very skilful tossing of the berries in flat wicker baskets, which separates all the husks to one end, and is fascinating to watch.

The incense godown was fascinating too, for its scents, for its colours, for its links with the past; from the Queen of Sheba whose prosperity had been based on the spice trade, to the Three Wise Men, whose gifts of frankincense and myrrh, the one from India and the other from Abyssinia or the Hadramaut, had been carried through the Red Sea or along the spice road which ran through the foothills on its eastern side. The trade in spices was still deeply mysterious and even A.B. professed to know little about it, but left the business to the one member of the staff who understood it; an uncommunicative Austrian who arranged shipments to obscure agencies in Balkan towns with unpronounceable names and at very little profit, since most of the currencies in which he was paid were blocked by exchange controls and could only be converted in the black market at a heavy discount.
'On the first floor is the upper office,' I continued,

> where the secretaries work, and some of their apartments. Then above that again are A.B's own quarters; he works sometimes here and sometimes below on the first floor. Further up the road is the garage, which does chiefly the firm's own work, on the ships etc., and on the first floor of this are more staff apartments. Then besides there is the soap factory at Ma'ala . . .

I had been put in Hides and Skins, and was

> trying to acquire some idea of the clerical work and the methods of keeping the various books in the department, but besides that I have spent a fair amount of time every day in

> the godown, watching the Arab sorters and weighers, and training my own eyes and hands in differentiating between a good and a bad skin – not at all an easy task ... Collins is going home on leave the week after I post this letter, and A.B. is not going to replace him, so I shall have to do all of his work I can without supervision, and the rest under A.B. Of course what I shall know at the end of three weeks will be hardly worth knowing, but it will be an ideal training.

Part of this training was to accompany the Arab buyer to the market in the old town where a few parcels of skins of inferior quality were to be picked up. Bidding for these was conducted in secret, buyer and seller linking their hands under cover of a turban and communicating through their fingers the prices that were asked and offered.

There were six of us in the men's mess, a former army barracks on the flat ground between the mountain and the sea. While the peninsula of Aden is mountainous, 'quite stupendously so', an early letter says,

> as soon as you get past that the country is, except for Little Aden (on the other side of the bay), flat desert until the hills of the Yemen, eighty miles to the north, and looking only fifteen as I can see them from where I write ... you can perhaps imagine what sort of place Aden must be for anyone who never goes into the hills, or out to sea, or only makes occasional journeys up-country – he would experience all the sensations of living on a small island, and that is actually what many people out here do find so oppressive.

The desert began beyond Sheikh Othman, where the firm stabled two Somali ponies,

> sturdy little beasts which will trot for hours without showing the least sign of tiring. We rode to a village to the north, over the desert which is here almost entirely flat, except for an occasional wadi, and is covered with small green bushes

which the camels eat but are of little value for anything else. Sheikh Othman itself is an oasis, i.e. a place where there is water near enough to the surface for the deep tap-roots of the date palm to reach it, but in this case there is running water as well, and there are gardens and cultivations. Outside the furthest village we rode to there was also cultivation of a sort. Bits of desert had been scraped and sowed in a haphazard manner, by what principles of selection I could not tell, as one looked just as dry as the next. The country is excellent for riding and we had some good gallops on the way back. You might think that because it was flat the country would be boring, but that is not so at all, and there is a great sense of space and freedom which would grow on one rapidly, I believe, and incidentally is an antidote to the opposite sensation I tried to describe above.

My usual companion on these occasions was Gale Read, the most likeable member of the mess, who had come to the firm of Besse via the Marseilles office and before that from the French foreign legion; a fine horseman, tough as nails, but without family or friends and desperately unsure of himself. A.B. affected to despise him, he loathed A.B. and most of his thoughts were how to leave the firm to join the Colonial police force, so that he could be back in the saddle again. He was full of hope, having been told by some clairvoyant to expect a vital change in the coming summer, which prediction was in fact fulfilled when he was killed in a motor accident. In the meanwhile he constantly talked of the day when he would be able to leave, while the two young graduates from St Andrews University who came out with me had already packed up and gone, after only a few months.

The Besses had among their friends a Mrs Ingrams, the wife of a political officer who appeared on rare occasions in Crater from his post in the Eastern Protectorate where he had just completed the first pacification of the warring tribes in the Hadramaut, an exciting world which seemed as far away from the tennis club and the Hides and Skins department as it had

Colonial Postscript

from London. The war in Abyssinia which I had come out hoping to see was equally remote. 'There were present two journalists,' I wrote of a party at the launching of one of our dhows,

> two of the many who left Addis in despair of ever finding out what was going on. Some of them have gone to British Somaliland, where they will not find anything either, some are at Aden, and one of these is on his way round through Egypt to the Sudan, while the other is a Pole who has managed to get permission to visit Massawa ... Hulls, whose name you will remember, is also to be sent there as the intermediary between the Shell company, whose agents we are, and the Italian government. If everything were to go according to plan – which it will not – he should be leaving again on November 18th, when there is bound to be a certain amount of anti-British feeling, that being the date of application of the final list of sanctions.

Four months later Aden was as far removed as ever from the centre of the stage. 'The authorities believe that the war in this part of the world is over,' I wrote disgustedly, 'for an official note has gone round the various stations that they are to consider themselves as constituted on a peace basis'.

In the meanwhile I had taken over the housekeeping arrangements in our bachelors' mess, and wrote a detailed account of them to my mother – news that would interest her and help to fill up a letter. There must have been something left over from my salary of £200 a year, since other letters describe various purchases including a rug in a diamond pattern of blue, still going strong after forty years, bought for the equivalent of thirty shillings. While the men looked after themselves, the female secretaries were quartered over the office, where they came under the firm's catering, but the arrangement had its disadvantages. 'The Besses,' I said in a letter home,

Aden, 1935–6

are inoculated against their own particular germ, and I very much doubt whether Mrs Besse ever goes near her own kitchen, though that does not prevent the two of them believing it to be the cleanest in Aden! (It is from hints like this that you must try to build up a picture of the 'House of Besse', as the Arabs call it – a phrase comprising firm, household, staff and the personality of the chief – as I shall never attempt to draw a complete character study.) They have a wonderfully efficient head boy, and it was to escape his clutches that we broke away. An efficiency that works entirely in the interests of someone else.

'You are quite right about Miss Hayes who was a secretary here,' I wrote later in reply to my mother, who was for ever curious about the female staff. 'She was one of the victims – there have been several – of the "House of Besse" food ... Irish and rather aloof; I have hardly exchanged a word with her. She could be quite a good-looker if she were to take the trouble but she doesn't try very hard'. In practice, I explained, 'the "Miss" is dropped, except by Hulls. The other secretary, as you are sure to be wanting to know, is Mrs Marek, or Petrushka, as she is always called for some reason, Russian, and married in some rather vague way, possibly divorced as well, I don't really know. She writes the French mail.' Indeed she wrote it brilliantly. Every week there would be a dozen or more letters of no more than a sentence or two to clients with whom the firm needed to keep in touch, but was not actually doing business at the moment, and each letter had a different turn of phrase, just right for the occasion, beautifully rounded, which made it glow like a tiny jewel among all the rest of the dull, impersonal English correspondence. 'Hayes is reputed to be keen on the Air Force, and so is Archer, but she is hardly one of the secretaries as she runs the coffee department and works downstairs with the rest of us'. But not for long. 'I told you I think that I have added Coffee to my other activities,' I wrote not long afterwards, 'and shall be entirely responsible for that as soon as Archer leaves in ten days time'.

Colonial Postscript

We had a terrific shipment from my department on Thursday, sending off 117 bales of one particular skin alone, and practically clearing out our stock in this sort. As this has not happened for a long time, there is a kind of stocktaking, and I found to my horror that we appeared to be about 1200 skins out, on the right side but that is not really any help, because it has got to be cleared up somehow or another, and the fault may lie in the dim past, long before J.M. was ever connected with skins. It is a difficult matter to trace here, because Arabs are inexact in their methods, and will be more than usually obscure when, as in this case probably, they have been cheating you somewhere. Because surely, if ever they saw an opportunity it would be now, when they have nothing but a greenhorn to contend with.

From last Thursday (28.11.35) until Christmas Day is the Mohammedan month of Ramadan, when from sunrise until sunset no bite of food or drop of water passes their lips. It is an observance to which they all adhere very strictly, and even quite young boys and old men undertake it. It is all very well for the rich Moslems, who can sleep most of the time, but for the coolies who have to work all day in the sun it can be terrible, and you may imagine what endurance they need when the month comes at midsummer. A number always die from the effects of it and I feel very sorry, even now, for the coolies working in the godown on the first day, when they feel the lack of food especially. They worked amazingly hard and cheerfully all the same. There is great excitement when the sun disappears and little parcels of dates are produced to break the fast. Groups form at the street corners for the common meal, and they sit talking and eating far into the night.

'I thought the photo would interest you,' I wrote a month or so later, 'though by now it is out of date. Two of the original six have already left, and two more are due to go shortly'. Among these was Drew Reid

Aden, 1935-6

who looks after the imports part of the work, and the infant soap factory, which is supposed to be ousting Levers from their trade in this part of the world (it is not very large!). Imports are very extensive, since we try to make all our branches selling as well as buying organisations, and so render them immune from the effects of currency fluctuations. The chief articles of trade are rice and sugar and "sheetings", the trade term for cotton goods, but there is a lot done in tea, galvanised iron, old newspapers, and of course the marketing of our own soap. In the mess we now have Lefebvre, who is in charge of the mechanical department, which handles several quite important agencies for trucks etc., which can be easily sold, and Hauser, the German, who looks after all the *Farbenindustrie* chemical, dyestuff and Agfa work, also quite a big affair. Collins will manage skins and hides, which is really the backbone of the firm's activities, but I shall continue in that as well as trying not to make too much of a mess of the coffee department, which is a more finicky business and requires a lot of attention to detail...

You ask about the coolies. Ours are well paid, because their labour is really quite skilled, and their foremen have considerable responsibility. So they are people with personality, though I must confess that only on rare occasions have I "got behind the face to the man". To start with I can't speak Arabic nearly well enough yet to make it easy, and besides I don't have occasion to speak to more than a few of them. Then, an Arab mentality is so utterly different from a European one, and until I've been here much longer I shall not begin to understand it. Most people only get as far as understanding relations and attitudes of mind of Arabs to themselves, i.e. Europeans, and with one another they are certainly quite different. A.B. is actually a person who does understand this very well, so much so that he behaves half-Arab himself. He lived among them so many years entirely alone that he got the opportunity to get to know their habits. He is always complaining that no one else ever takes the trouble to understand them.

Colonial Postscript

Skins came over from the Somali coast in vast numbers, usually in our own dhows which in favourable sailing conditions would outpace the Cowasjee Dinshaw steamers that ran between Aden and Djibouti. Mostly they were goatskins destined for the glove makers of Yeovil and Milan, or the heavier grade skins of the fat-tailed Somali sheep. But there were also kidskins, including those of unborn kids with tight curled hair which would probably be passed off as Persian lamb, and leopardskins, which were in a class by themselves. They varied from the Abyssinian skins with heavy fur and dark markings to the much lighter skin with a more distinctive marking from the lower plateau of British Somaliland. Finest of all were those from the hinterland of Mogadishu, in Italian Somaliland, where the desert or semi-desert conditions and intense heat had induced the lightest of all skins, both in weight and in colour; in fact they were almost lacking in spots except for a delicately graded pattern over the shoulders and along the ridge of the back. These arrived not in batches but as single skins, brought across to Aden by a Somali agent of the hunter, or even the hunter himself. Such skins might fetch between Rs140–160 (£10–12). Four would be needed to make a coat, the value of which today would be many thousands of pounds, if still to be had at all. Even in those days they were rarely seen, and Collins told us how he had pursued a coat half-way across New York before he had been able to convince himself that it was top quality, and its wearer that his interest in it was merely technical. The hunters knew their value too and followed the animals for days, at great personal risk, until the opportunity presented itself for a spear thrust in the neck or throat, which would kill the animal without damaging its skin. These Somalis were arrogant, magnificent creatures. Tall and spare, the men were too angular to be truly handsome, but their women were beautiful and walked with a superb carriage. The purchase of a valuable Somali leopardskin was a dramatic affair in which most of the office soon became involved, ending with the wild man from the desert accepting our bid – at best a paltry return for a venture on which he had staked his life – or rejecting it

Aden, 1935-6

disdainfully and taking his merchandise to a rival firm down the road.

Lefebvre, who had now joined our mess, was an enterprising Frenchman and fluent Arab speaker who had no intention of remaining cooped up in the Aden peninsula and, being in charge of the transport department, had means of organizing trips outside it. The first of these was to Dhala, one of the independent principalities in the Protectorate perched on one of those high foothills of the Yemen whose outlines I had observed with longing even in the first hours after arrival. Dhala is beautifully described in a short account by Freya Stark which appeared first in *The Times* and was afterwards reprinted in one of her books. Ours was a different kind of journey, having to be crammed into the space between the closing of the office at noon on Saturday and the distribution of the European mail on Sunday evening. 'The journeys up and down took well over half the total time,' I wrote. There were six of us, with a representative of the bus owner, a servant and a guard, bringing the total strength to nine.

> Total strength is the right word, as there were many times when all the man-power available was needed to extricate the bus from situations which it is quite impossible to imagine if you picture the road as having anything in common with an English one – or the bus either! The most difficult part of the route was that lying in the wadi bed, beyond Lahej. As rains fill it very seldom, you can see roughly where the track goes, but the gravel is so loose that you may still get stuck and everyone has to get out to shove clear, or you may have to pick your own line over or between large boulders. The last stage of the journey started after dark, and it was in pitch blackness and a fine drizzle that we began to climb out of the gorge, as the wadi bed had now become. About half-way up we were all out and shoving to help the wheels get some sort of purchase on the rocks and loose stones, but in spite of that it ran onto a boulder which snapped the exhaust pipe clean at the base and squashed the petrol feed pipe flat. A less pleasant

place for running repairs could hardly be imagined. Through the mist we could just see a projecting pinnacle of rock and the whole scene looked wild in the extreme. Fortunately machinery, which ceases to have any interest for me the moment it ceases to go, apparently begins to exercise its appeal to others at the same moment, and after 1½ hours work Lefebvre and Cox got it going again. Shoving behind, we got to the top, where we finally arrived at about 1.30 a.m. It says a good deal for the Dhala air, and something for the hardness of a concrete floor that we were all up again at 6.30, to see the sun come up over a magnificent landscape of range after range of hills, with the village on the hill side, built up against it in much the same way as the photographs you must have seen of Tibetan houses. The air was cool and wonderfully exhilarating after Aden. We ate most of our food for breakfast, since the Emir had sent us a present of a sheep, which we watched being dissected in a very professional manner. We had it later for lunch, and it was tender as chicken.

In a separate enclosure I am going to send you the presents for Roger and David (my younger brothers) which I bought in Dhala – two slings which are used for shooting birds when they come to the wadis in wet weather. You put a round pebble in the little bag at the end and whirl it round your head. If you release one of the ends the stone will fly with practice to a distance of well over 100 yards, and at a short distance they can be most accurate – and deadly, as Goliath found to his cost! I wish I could send you one of the other things I bought, a gourd filled with honey, but I'm afraid it wouldn't travel . . . It was a great trip, and a most interesting one – few people except the political officers have made it, so the place is really unspoilt.

More and more as the days passed it became clear that they, and not the dealers in hides and skins, were the people privileged to see the wide, wide world!

Besides the Somali ponies out at Sheikh Othman, A.B. – who

Aden, 1935–6

seems to have had some very British notions about the virtues of fresh air and exercise – also owned a sailing dhow which for some reason was looked after by the R.A.F. doctor and had been converted by him into a Bermuda-rigged ketch. The doctor's bungalow at Tarshyne was a haven 'and you can perhaps understand,' I wrote, 'what it means to be able to go to a home where I am always welcome, can always have a meal or spend the night, or accept any hospitality which is always given in the completely unself-conscious open-handed Irish style, which makes it so easy to accept'. In the *Dharifa* we would sail over to Little Aden, now the site of a big oil refinery but then a fishing village, stay Saturday night camped there, and then sail back to Aden to be in time for the arrival of the mail on Sunday. Like some 40 of the firm's lighters, she had been built at Ma'ala 'supposed to be the oldest dhow-building yard in the Red Sea, turning out ships on order for the Queen of Sheba, and for many others before and since'.

> Last week we launched there the *Mufid* – the "useful" one – the largest dhow ever to leave the Aden stocks, and no Clydeside crowd ever watched a launching with greater interest than did the inhabitants of Ma'ala, with the difference that in this case the success of the operation was largely dependent on their own efforts. She was too big to go down one slipway, and so was built on three, and had to be moved sideways into the water. It was a long job – two hours to shift her about 50 yards into a position where she would float off when the tide rose. The haulers could not keep her moving for more than a few feet at a time, and then the jacks had to be fixed against the hull and set the whole bulk moving again.

> A week later, 'A.B. says he is going up to Addis on his way home to Europe, travelling to Djibouti in the new dhow the *Mufid* on her maiden voyage, though as she is at the moment stuck fast in the mud instead of floating off properly he won't be able to unless we get an unusually high tide in the near future. I'm sure he wants to show everyone how brave he is, since there

is a good chance of either Addis or the railway being bombed shortly'. In fact this happened only a day or two later. The Italians had already attacked Djidjigah and 'we have no precise news of the damage but I suspect that goods in our branch to the value of Rs30,000 went up in smoke, and probably with a bang as well, since part of it was Shell benzene and kerosene. Our agent is reported to be safe, in British territory. Commerce seems occasionally to have its thrills'. Summer had now started, and A.B. was away to Europe. This was a great day.

I saw A.B. off on the *El Haq* yesterday afternoon. We went on board and waited there till the mail arrived from the *Viceroy of India*. An impressive collection, a pile of letters three or four feet high, bearing the postage stamps of countries all over the world – especially the more disreputable ones, as someone remarked. They were sorted out hurriedly into the different departments and A.B. read through the more important ones with Collins and the chief Indian accountant, Goring and I surreptitiously digesting our letters from home in the meantime. We then went back, waving good-bye from the launch. The old rogue! He is a scoundrel, but one cannot help liking and admiring him.

'A.B., whose name is like gold in this country,' wrote Freya Stark of Wadi Do'an in the distant Hadramaut, which she visited the year previously. In these remote towns where each window of every house had a hole below and behind it for the barrel of a gun, Government was a transitory force, coming sometimes from this quarter and sometimes from that, uncertain and unreliable in its operation, not like the House of Besse in Aden, for which every trader was a client and every man of substance an ambassador. There was a stir when any of these minor potentates visited the office. Unknown to us but fascinating figures, they were escorted between the desks of the coffee department and the skins department to the upstairs saloon where A.B., like the great merchant prince that he was, perhaps the last of his line, would entertain them with easy familiarity

Aden, 1935–6

and perfect knowledge of their customs, their background and their language, acquired in a lifetime of experience of Southern Arabia. Probably all they talked about was the price of sugar and sheetings but the ritual was highly impressive and, no doubt, commercially very rewarding.

With other nationalities he seemed less at ease, always excepting those of every race who, because of some iron in their own characters, found themselves responding to his personal magnetism. A.B. shunned the European community, deploring its idle ways, its lack of self-discipline, its uneducated tastes – or so we gathered from his interpreters, particularly Mme Besse, rather than from the great man himself. In retrospect one can find in this attitude some reflection of an early struggle for existence which must have been exceptionally severe. Like other such men he had a great, and to those who possessed it and took it for granted, an exaggerated respect for education – it was an immense feather in his cap that he, the poor boy made good, was able to attract and bring back with him to a country where high educational qualifications were rarely found, no less than three graduates from famous British universities. But before twelve months were up he had lost them all again, as he had lost staff before and was to lose others later, while the firm continued to grind along with the old faithful, the nucleus of men who, lacking in either vision or intellect, at least understood well enough the basic principle on which his and all other commercial empires have been founded, that big profits are only to be made on low costs.

And so in 1935, and through the uneasy years that followed, the undistinguished building that was the material House of Besse stood in the centre of the dusty old town, with the goats wandering in from the street to the shade of the godown at midday, and the sorters in the godown, as the daylight began to fail, continuing their work among the goats in the street, while the owner of the business, dividing his time between Europe in the summer and Aden in the winter, but taking it with him wherever he went, accumulated first his million and then his multimillions, paying no taxes – for Aden was a free port – and,

Colonial Postscript

I was told years later, dying just a few days before its Estate Duty Ordinance passed into law, so depriving the government of a fortune which this law had been specially designed to catch. But that was not the end of the story.

Like his great compatriot, General de Gaulle, A.B. was a lover of France but had a low opinion of most Frenchmen. England he hated but the English, or at least a few of them, he admired and always spoke of with respect. This respect, coupled with that for education, must have led to the decision to leave a large part of his great wealth for the establishment and endowment of a college, St Antony's at Oxford. Thus, he may have argued to himself, he would discharge his duty to society, completely and also dramatically, in a manner which would render him equal to the greatest benefactors of learning in the past. A satisfying thought.

All this lay years ahead. In the meanwhile there was the usual mail with the invoices and statements of account and bills of lading to be made out for our posts in Abyssinia, where the victorious Italian army had just reached Addis, and agents in British, French and Italian Somaliland, Egypt, Eritrea, Saudi Arabia, the Yemen and Makalla, not to mention Japan, India, the United States and all other countries whose letters had been cascading over the stateroom floor. With the departure of A.B. all the former urgency disappeared and we became, almost overnight, just like what one supposed any other business might have been. As the miles lengthened, as the days passed, the sense of involvement lessened. It was an agreeable change, but also disturbing. Just then another trip out of Aden materialized, this time to Shuqra.

Shuqra lies east of Aden, along the coast. It was another fascinating though hurried journey, away from the now uninspired routine of the office, meeting people who were people and not just customers, and only the underfed goats recalled unhappily the skins one would be sorting the following morning. This was the moment of truth. 'It seems likely to be my last trip in Arabia, for some time at any rate, and I greatly enjoyed it,' was all I said in a guarded letter home, but by the same mail

Aden, 1935-6

there went another to the Colonial Office, asking still to be considered for an appointment as a political officer in the Colonial Service, for which I had already had some interviews in the previous year. A few days later I spoke to Collins, despising myself for doing so in A.B.'s absence, and gave him my resignation. I remember he was not surprised.

Note

Antonin Besse died at Gordonstoun, Elgin, on 2 July 1951, at the age of 74. His obituary notice (*The Times*, 5.7.51) is almost totally unrevealing about his past career and deals mainly with his benefactions to Oxford. These had been made three years previously, at the time anonymously, and consisted of £1.25 million for the new foundation of St Antony's and £.25 million for improvements at eight other colleges: Lincoln, Exeter, Worcester, Wadham, St Peter's Hall, St Edmund Hall, Pembroke and Keble, chiefly with the object of enabling them to accommodate more French students. Besse at first declined but later accepted the distinction of a Doctor of Civil Law at the University of Oxford, and he was also awarded a K.B.E. – Honorary, because during all his years in a British colony he had never surrendered his French citizenship.

Other benefactions of his to this country are the two beautiful carvings from Shabwa which adorn the small room in the British Museum dedicated to South Arabian art.

In 1976 I had lunch with Mr A. J. Footman, a former member of St Antony's College, who had been commissioned by Mme Besse after her husband's death to write his biography. The task occupied him three years, during which he visited Aden on several occasions, interviewed members of A.B.'s family, former employees and other associates, and was able to unravel – with some gaps – the remarkable history of this remarkable man and of the firm he founded.

As the work proceeded, Mme Besse (an Englishwoman, and A.B.'s one-time secretary) became more and more unhappy about the direction it was taking. She had intended a hagiography, but Besse had been no saint, and her wishes would have been impossible to fulfil. So the manuscript remained locked away, while the old lady lived on, healthy and active, running the small estate of Le Paradou in Provence, pruning her vines, and occupied with her vast store of memories. Then at last the time came when she could no longer impose her will, and the biography was published (*Antonin Besse of Aden*, David Footman, St Antony's/Macmillan 1980), but it lifts only some of the veils surrounding his character.

II
Northern Nigeria – Sokoto, 1937–8

The 1936 list of appointments to the Colonial Service was published in the late summer, when the new cadets began at either Oxford or Cambridge a course of training in their future responsibilities. The emphasis was on law, language and anthropology, but the course included lectures on tropical hygiene and field surveying. These last two subjects were a relic of the times, disappearing but not yet gone for good, when departmental specialists were few on the ground and a district officer with the time and inclination could carry out his own programme of minor public works – and quite remarkable some of them were! Roads, bridges and buildings were essential to a good administration, and so of course were water supplies. The students bicycled out in groups to a field at the back of the University bathing sheds to assist in a demonstration of how to drive a borehole but, though the site was only a few yards from the Cam, the instructor warned us that the exercise would yield no water. 'Not suitable soil,' he said enigmatically, leaving us to wonder how such an explanation would go down with an audience of expectant and probably thirsty Africans. He also showed us how to tie a hangman's knot 'just in case you need it', adding with a note of some regret 'though that sort of thing has rather gone out nowadays, I believe'.

My posting was to Northern Nigeria. This may have been due to the fact that I had by this time acquired some rudiments of Arabic, and that Arabic is spoken in a part of the country, though not the part to which I was eventually despatched. My destination was Sokoto Province (pronounced like 'cockatoo'), up in the northwest corner, an area rich in history, for it was here that the last of the five great empires which rose and fell in the Sudan between the 8th and 20th centuries had been founded; it lasted, as had been foretold, for precisely a hundred years and finally collapsed to a handful of British-led troops in 1903. Even today, arrival there still counts as one of my most memorable experiences. It was a journey of some 700 miles from the coast which, before there was any wheeled transport, had taken the political officers of a former generation three weeks, but now it took only two or three days. The train jogged all night through the rain forest and on during the next day through mile after mile of seemingly endless bush, of trees for the most part not more than twenty or thirty feet in height. It was an enclosed country which revealed no pattern or purpose, to the newcomer at any rate, and it continued well into the southern part of Sokoto Province itself. Then about 25 miles short of Sokoto the scenery changed dramatically. The bush thinned out and all at once the eye acquired a new perspective. Northwards lay a vast expanse of undulating country, now fresh and green after the rains, with here a party of horsemen threading its way down some distant track, there the smoke of a hidden fire, and ahead the long stretch of the red laterite road – for we had left railhead far behind and were travelling the last hundred miles or so in the Government lorry, myself in the privileged seat next to the driver and behind, mixed up with the mail and official stores of all descriptions, my newly acquired servants, bed, bath, filter, cooking chest, saddlery, library and provisions from John Holt's store in Lagos. This broad expanse of plain we were now entering continued to the north until it merged insensibly with the arid fringes of the Sahara and, on either side, stretched with little variation of scenery or vegetation from Senegal 1500 miles to the west, and through the Anglo-Egyptian Sudan to the mountains of Eritrea and Abyssinia 3000 miles to the east. Here was room and to spare, a contrast with Aden that was both superb and exciting.

Northern Nigeria – Sokoto, 1937–8

The road to the capital ran along the edge of the European station, marked by notices, a golf course and thatched bungalows secluded in their sandy compounds behind oleander bushes and straggling gold-mohur. No signs of life however, for blissfully deprived of telephones and communication with higher authority in the south, Sokoto kept its own hours, rose a little earlier in the morning and knocked off for the day after a late lunch, to sleep as nature intended. Fortunately the driver knew the drill and deposited me with my loads and servants in one of the two empty resthouses, a large hut consisting of a single room and verandah all the way round it, with thick mud walls and a grass roof suspended over the top like a giant umbrella, supported on a circle of wooden poles, up which the white ants daily constructed fresh tunnels, which daily had to be removed. This was my new home and, it later transpired, being a 'bush house' qualified the occupant under Nigerian General Orders for an allowance of £3 a month, sufficient to pay the cook's wages, and nearly enough to buy an untrained pony.

There was an established procedure for dealing with newly appointed cadets, who were usually posted for their first six months to the Provincial Office, where they came directly under the Resident and had a chance to find their feet, while learning how the machinery of government worked. Until they had acquired a knowledge of the language, it was about the only place where they could be usefully employed. In an area almost as big as England, with a population of nearly two million Africans, and a mere dozen political officers, it seemed only common sense for the administrative processes, in so far as they involved Africans, to be conducted in their language. This applied not only to oral communications but to written court proceedings and records of account, where indeed the modern 'Arabic' numerals had not yet displaced the 'Ajami' or ancient Arabic script in many of the outlying districts. So Hausa, which is a rich and vivid language with a wide vocabulary, was spoken universally and often with great fluency by Europeans, particularly the administrative staff. Proficiency in language was one of the factors in rating for promotion, but this was the least of the reasons for acquiring it. Knowledge of the idiom, the customs to which it often referred and the folklore so interwoven with their lives led to a fuller understanding of the mentality of the African population, and to a more accurate appreciation of what needed to be and what could be done to improve their situation. The strength of the British influence in Northern Nigeria rested not on force to back its presence, since this was negligible, but on the acceptability of its actions, either because they were obviously well-founded or, in the last resort, because of the prestige of those who directed them. Instances of this will be given later but I will just mention here the example of Mai-farin-kai (the one with the fair hair – everyone had his nickname) a British officer of the old days who, after the Satiru rebellion, had ridden out to the village which was the site of the engagement, caused a furrow to be driven through the site and sown it with salt. A generation later this piece of ground remained uncultivated, and the people spoke of the act with veneration. In this case, massive retribution would not have achieved a result one-tenth as effective as this simple dramatic gesture, so well calculated to appeal to the imagination of those who witnessed it.

'My first two days have been spent in the Provincial Office which is in charge of a man called Mant,' I wrote, going on to explain that he was an administrative cadet of the previous years' intake.

> This morning however, I went up to the Resident's office where I swore allegiance and fealty to George VI, as directed by the Acting Resident, who just beat me playing tennis later this evening. He leaves in a few days when the Resident – John Carrow – returns from leave in England. After that I drove with him and the D.O. Sokoto – Backhouse – to the palace of the Sarkin Mussulmi (this was the Sultan), a genial old boy, in magnificent but rather dirty robes. He sat in state in a chair with the Wazir (Vizier) and a few of the Council ranged along the floor by his side, who put in a word occasionally but for the most part were content to remark

Northern Nigeria – Sokoto, 1937–8

"Gaskiya ne" – "It is the truth" (which it probably wasn't) when some remark of the Sultan's seemed to call for it. We sat in chairs opposite.

The letter went on to describe the ceremonial of the visit, the meeting and the escorts, but of course it missed many finer points of custom and etiquette of which I would have been more conscious on a later occasion. The Fulani aristocracy in Northern Nigeria though capable of acting with enormous vigour when there was real need for it set great store by civilized behaviour in ordinary intercourse. The possession of 'Hankali' or 'Hankuri', which might be variously translated as 'care', 'consideration' or 'decorum' was one of their highest terms of praise. 'Hankuri maganin duniya,' says one of their proverbs, the sense of which is not very far removed from that of the Wykhamist motto 'Manners makyth man'. All conversations between educated persons began with mutual enquiries about health, strength and disposition, and these were no mere formality. They ended with similar courtesies. 'May you dismount in peace,' were the last words a rider would hear when departing on a journey, to which his reply would be 'Amen. May God bring it to pass.' Divine providence was never out of mind, and a future intention would never be uttered without being qualified by the phrase 'if God wills'.

Decisions about future postings, including that of the new cadet, had to await Carrow's return. In the meanwhile I was attached to various officers to see what sort of work was being done by them; to Mant to help him with a surprise check of the Native Treasury, and to Backhouse when he inspected the N.A. Prison. N.A. stood for Native Administration. There were six of these in the Province, of which Sokoto was easily the biggest, and the whole of Northern Nigeria was covered with a network of them, large and small. In each case the administration was carried out, not in the name of George VI but of the Native Authority whom George VI (via the proper channels of course!) had recognised. The Authority might be a chief, or a chief in council, or a council, depending on local tradition or historical accident, arising from the fact that the divisions of territory and incidence of power in 1937 were still to a great extent as we had found them in 1903, apart from a few later modifications. These authorities varied considerably in status; in the large and important ones like Sokoto the powers held were very far-reaching and included, for example, the power of life and death in the court of the Chief Alkali, and the power of the Sultan to cause the sentence to be carried out, according to Mohammedan law, by his own executioner – though as this officer was somewhat out of practice the sentence was usually carried out by the government hangman at Kaduna. The vital role of these native authorities will be appreciated from the fact that they undertook the assessment and collection of taxes, a substantial part of which was retained by them to meet the requirements of their own administration. 'It's all down in the text books,' I explained somewhat lazily to my mother, who was extremely unlikely to have Lugard's *Dual Mandate* on her shelves, 'and means for instance, in the case of the prison, that instead of training our own nominees, who would run it efficiently, we work through the Sultan's representative and thus have to put up with a good deal of inefficiency and waste. It would be very much easier to do it ourselves,' I continued, with all the wealth of a week or two's experience, 'but in the long run it would be fatal to the accepted policy of trying to make the natives do it for themselves, and when I see or hear the progress that has been made already I'm very much less sceptical about this than when I was in England.'

Another excursion was with the Veterinary Officer to a rinderpest immunization camp west of Sokoto.

> All the cattle owners are Fulani, some of whom understand Hausa, and they are continually on the move with their stock as the pastures give out. They have a sort of working arrangement with the Hausa farmers who are settled people and allow the cattle to graze in return for their valuable manure. The Fulani were originally a conquering race and their blood runs in the ruling Hausa families; there are very

Northern Nigeria – Sokoto, 1937–8

handsome faces among them in a womanly and quite un-Negroid sort of way ... Other work that the Veterinary Department does is to improve the method of hide-drying and the breed of goats which supply the famous leather called "Moroccan" because it used to be taken all the way over the Sahara to the ports in the Mediterranean, there having been no communication with the South in the old days.

The method of improving the breed of goat was simply that of castrating all the males that were not of the right colour, and this was one of the many matters on which touring officers were supposed to comment in their reports – I recall one of these facetiously remarking that those which remained entire seemed to be undertaking their additional duties conscientiously! Goats wandered at large about the streets and alleyways of Sokoto, as they had done in Aden, adding to the general untidiness. With Backhouse I went to the Thursday market, a famous one that was attended weekly by thousands of people, some of them from far afield in French territory, as well as traders from all parts of British Nigeria. The District Officer was an enthusiast for improved sanitation – and indeed there was plenty of scope for it. Fairly soon I found myself carrying out my first engineering work 'supervising the building of nine public conveniences in the market with prison labour – these the populace may, or may not be persuaded to use, instead of the more convenient side of the road – I hope to be up there on market day to see if they are proving at all popular'. My mother must have passed some comment, for a letter a few weeks later provided further explanation. 'I must have misled you, to imagine that I've been building W.C.s Far from it! E. is universal here, the nearest W. being at least two hundred miles away. Plug-pulling, didn't you know it, is one of the recognised joys of the Colonial newly home on leave in England?'

Were it not for these faithfully preserved letters home the present chapters would not only be half their length, but also less authentic. Their value is what they have recalled to mind, as well as what they recorded. In a book published in 1969, called

Colonial Postscript

The British in Northern Nigeria, the author Robert Heussler observes after having read a good many letters (filed as these have been in the Rhodes Library at Oxford) that they are often 'couched in the special language that dutiful sons use with mothers who must be protected by a film of mythology from the real world's harshness'. There is some truth in the observation; letters certainly do not give the whole story. But they also reveal many things that are unexpected, when re-read for the first time more than thirty years later. Some of these things are about Africa, some about oneself. The chips begin to show again through the gloss that memory had acquired with age, and one realizes for the first time that it may not have been so much that Africa was remarkable as that it was being viewed through the eyes of one who was in his early twenties.

Heussler's book deals with a period in Nigerian history rather earlier than mine, and at a higher level than that of the newly arrived cadet. One of its heroes is Carrow, the Resident of Sokoto Province who had now newly returned from leave. He was the 'babban Bature', or 'big white chief', and big he was both in size and personality. He immediately decided that I should do my stint in the Provincial Office later in the year, after some initial touring in the districts nearer to the capital, the 'Home Counties' as they were called, to distinguish them from the more distant 'Shires', or the semi-pagan areas to the south referred to as the 'Celtic fringe'. In the following chapter I shall have to depart at times from the strict chronological sequence, which might give a rather confusing picture. It will be mainly about life on tour, and after that I shall be back again, just before Christmas, for a longish spell at headquarters.

However, one must start with the Provincial Office, if only briefly, since that and the Resident's office a quarter of a mile away was really the hub around which the whole province revolved. It was an unpretentious and very ordinary 'temporary' building ('il n'y a rien qui dure comme le provisoire') in all respects except one, which was a brass tablet on the verandah wall recording the first visit to Sokoto by the explorer Clapperton and his death there in 1827. Inside with both windows open sat

Northern Nigeria – Sokoto, 1937–8

the A.D.O. in charge, dressed in coat and tie whatever the weather, cursing the heat but at the same time secretly proud of the fact that, because of its unique Resident, this was the only province where the formalities were observed. Behind him the strongroom, of which he was one of the three key-holders; there being no bank in Sokoto where the Government could open an account it had to look after the cash itself, and when the tax came in there were bags and bags of it, each of £100 in brown West African Currency Board shillings, bound with red tape and with a label on the neck of the bag, certifying its contents and signed by whoever had counted them. This certificate was not only as to the quantity of coin but also as to its genuineness – and that is quite a story. 'During the past two or three months,' I was to write later

> we have been sending large remittances of specie down to Zaria, amounting actually to £55,000, and on each they have reported large sums of counterfeit coins, with a certain amount of shortage as well. They arise out of sealed bags of £100 each which we receive as share of Government tax from the Native Treasuries in the province and are usually forwarded with seals unbroken. We've been having a long and wordy battle with various authorities from the Accountant-General downwards to decide who will have to make good the deficiency (at present charged as personal advances to Roberts and myself) and this is not finished yet. In the meanwhile we are sending down a further £5000 and as this is a comparatively small sum we decided to count it and check it ourselves. So I closed the office for all business on Friday and until 12 o'clock on Saturday, put chairs and tables out on the verandah and Cole, Mant, Costello (Forestry), two representatives of the Native Treasury and myself sat down to count the money and check every single coin to see if it was a dud. Nearly all of it was in shillings which meant 100,000 coins to be examined. Some of the counterfeits are so good that it is almost certain a few got through, but we found £4/12/– spurious coinage. From the face they are almost

undetectable except to scrutiny under a magnifying glass, and the only practicable test is that of milling. Twenty shillings are counted out and placed in a pile, laid out between thumb and finger and rolled over – a counterfeit may then show up owing to its being slightly thicker than the rest, or smaller in size, or the milling may be on the slant, or broken at the edges, or slightly irregular – you get to recognise the different kinds – the first for instance was evidently minted in large quantities in 1936. Apart from the finding of duds the counting and examining is extremely tedious, and only relieved by the discovery of a particularly difficult specimen, such as the last for instance, where the break may occur at only one point in the circumference and the coin is otherwise perfect. The work is rendered more difficult by the fact that there is no such thing as a standard coin, the 1920 shillings have widely spaced milling with edges having a worn appearance, and more recent issues are much more closely milled. The coin is all very dirty and one's hands finish up a disgusting greeny-brown colour! It is alloy, the silver issues were not made after 1920 and are now almost all withdrawn from circulation. I withdraw whatever there is that comes in. In those days people hadn't the skill to do counterfeiting and besides it wouldn't have been so profitable as it is now with a base metal coinage of low intrinsic value. At the time when it was brought in the natives didn't like the alloy at all – now they won't take silver. About half the silver shillings were English, many of them from 1893 which you don't often meet at home. You see what a different economy we have to that which exists in Europe – except for Government and the firms there are no paper transactions, trade is on a cash basis and the cash is almost all coin, for the average native would hardly have occasion to want so large a sum as 10/– once in a lifetime.

A month later; 'I told you about the last £5000 we counted and checked ourselves before sending it down to Zaria. They found 12/– more, the shortage as usual being debited as a personal advance to the Local Treasurer, but the Resident very sportingly

Northern Nigeria – Sokoto, 1937–8

found the 12/– himself and cleared me, so whoever it is that will have to find the difference this time it won't be J. Morley once in a way!'

The verandah outside the office was normally occupied by the Government messengers, robed and turbaned, whose low hum of voices died away as the day wore on or one of them retired, enamel kettle in hand, to perform his ritual ablutions. These were the trusted retainers, who came and went, doubling their duty on the office steps with that of accompanying officers on tour. All but illiterate, they had for compensation prodigious memories of all that had been said or done in the province during the last 20 years, and were a mine of information about its remotest tracks and villages. By contrast the clerks in the office, all of whom had come up from the south, mission-educated Christians, unhappy exiles in the midst of an alien Mohammedan majority, unable to get the food or drink to which they were accustomed, seemed able to remember nothing at all about the past. 'It must be written down somewhere,' they said and would produce hopefully, but without conviction a venerable file, the paper of which was brown with age and so brittle from the alternate damp and dryness of the atmosphere that corners broke off the pages as one turned them over, looking for the elusive precedent, the red-inked Residential ruling of days gone by. Sometimes the telephone rang, but it was always a family affair if it did, the D.O. Birnin Kebbi to report a swarm of locusts flying eastwards and to ask if there was any butter in the cold store. Or it might be Carrow, nominally to raise a point on a file which had just reached him but in reality because he was bored with the isolation of his own office and wanted to vary it with some conversation. Outside there was little traffic in the sun-drenched square, where a casual wind raised dust-devils over its sandy surface but then, thinking better of it, allowed them to die away again. Through the other window lay the golf course, endowed by some energetic predecessor with an avenue of untidy yellow-blossomed cassia trees, leading to the old fort now crumbling into ruins and hardly more than a mound. Beyond that again the club and the gardens, the Education Officer's bungalow, the Conservator of Forests' bungalow, and then the Nigerian bush, stretching away to anywhere or nowhere, the nearest thing to infinity in my experience. There is an appropriate story – in Africa there is always the appropriate story – of the junior officer who was asked by his Resident to produce an outline plan for a new Government station and did so, very neatly, with the roads marked, and the site of the bungalows, and the polo ground and the offices.

'Splendid,' said the Resident, 'but what are these initials, M.M.A., in each of the four corners?'

'Oh, those!,' said the junior officer, 'sorry I forgot to explain, they stand for miles and miles of Africa.'

III
Northern Nigeria – Sokoto continued, 1937–8

In reality, this vast expanse of Africa was neither anonymous nor as featureless as it appeared. There were indeed miles and miles of low plateau country where the soil was no more than a light red dusting on the rock or the subterranean water lay too deep for the professional well diggers (a sub-tribe called the Arawa) to reach it. To my eyes, one stretch of this country looked identical with the next. To a native's it would have its own individuality, and he would run not the slightest risk of being lost there. Out of this 'bush' the paths always emerged, eventually, onto farmland. The fields here were small and totally unfenced, except for an occasional barrier of thorns to protect a special patch of cassava or sweet potato, growing in a damper piece of ground. The main crops were bulrush millet, which did better in the sandy areas with the lighter rainfall, and Guinea corn which seemed to need a heavier soil; its stalks had to make eight to ten feet of growth in the season and after harvest were tied together in bundles to be used as 'rafters' for thatching. Just before the harvest it was possible to be on horseback and still not see over the tops of them. Only the land nearest to the village was farmed continuously, where it could be manured with refuse from the town or by arrangement with the Fulani cattle owners. The rest was shifting cultivation, which meant that a patch could only be used for a few years until it lost fertility, when a new area had to be cleared in the dry season by burning all the trees and undergrowth. But some trees would always be spared and were indeed safeguarded by

Native Administration orders; these included such trees as the 'doruwa', or locust bean, the best shade tree of them all, whose fruit hanging in ungainly pods was used as an ingredient in soup, or baobabs whose bark was peeled off in long strips for rope making.

To one riding through the open fields in the dry season after the harvest a patch of treetops on the horizon betrayed the presence of a town or village long before the roofs themselves became visible. According to my companions it had been a deliberate policy in the old days to plant up the area where the houses lay, so that a party of raiders seeing the trees from afar might judge the settlement to be larger than it was and turn aside. It was difficult to believe that the Hausa people and their neighbours had ever been so far-sighted on the one hand or so easily deceived on the other! But this sort of talk was a reminder that the old days of warfare were not forgotten and in particular Umaru, the messenger at my side, was always pointing out the site of some former bloody engagement, and enlarging on its memories.

However, this insecurity had brought some compensations, for the exposed countryside of the north forced its inhabitants to come together for safety and not, as in forested or hilly areas, to seek it in dispersal. In the towns and cities they founded, the arts of civilization had been brought to a high pitch even though, as is generally the case with pre-industrial societies, most of the population had to be occupied most of the time in satisfying the daily needs of the community, and only a minority enjoyed the benefits of leisure.

In the larger villages or those which had been staging posts along well-frequented routes there was often a European rest house, that is to say the usual round house with a number of smaller huts at the back of it, standing apart from the native town, where the delicately nurtured white man could get some relief from the drumming and barking of dogs that went on through the night (however drumming could be curtailed while the dogs could be – and often were – rounded up and taken out to 'bush' for the occasion). More often though there were no special quarters, and in these cases one of the villagers had to be evacuated from his

Northern Nigeria – Sokoto continued, 1937–8

home so that it could be occupied by the travelling District Officer and his staff, all the owner's belongings being removed and the compound swept out and prepared for the visitor. Incidentally, these preparations included the digging and rigging of an E.C. in what was fondly imagined to be the European style – though often more suitable for an acrobat. The routine of touring went like this. Everything had to be securely packed so that it could be head loaded by carriers from one stopping place to the next, and in those days there was no difficulty in recruiting the 15 to 20 men required. The job was completed after supper, so that the carriers, who slept during the day, could start off at 2 a.m., or midnight, or even 10 p.m. if they had a long march in front of them. Last item to be packed was the chair in which one was sitting and the book one was reading. Only the 'small boy' with one carrier stayed behind until the following morning to make a cup of tea and to load up bed, mosquito net, pyjamas and so on, a bulky load but not a particularly heavy one, which meant that they did not get in until the afternoon and the last part of their march had to be done in the midday sun. When these arrangements worked, as they nearly always did, one arrived to find a bath full of cold water, clean clothes laid out and the kettle on the fire – and very agreeable this was, after travelling for many, many hours, not necessarily by the direct route of the carriers, for there would be people to be seen and things to be done on the way. Undoubtedly the best moment of the day was submerging one's body from neck to thigh, as much as could be accommodated at one time, in the oval tin bath, 'and woe betide the boy who comes along with a cracked teapot at that moment,' I wrote. The carriers got 6d a day when at work, with a bonus of a penny or two when their journey was more than 17 miles, and 3d a day when they were resting; however they never drew more than the minimum rate, the balance being banked for them until their return to base. There were some unexpected hazards, the memory of which returns sharply to mind on re-reading a letter to my sister.

Earwigs . . . Every now and then I reach a rest house which is full of them, and they invade all my loads; during the

Colonial Postscript

following days, as new books, clothes etc. are produced out of the boxes they are slaughtered one by one and the tribe is gradually reduced, until we reach the point when hardly any are left. About the same time, of course, we are certain to reach another infested rest house, and the hunt begins all over again. My loads go ahead of me every night and when I dress in the morning (this would be before dawn) there is only a mat in the middle of the floor with the 'bare necessities' of shaving kit, clothes etc., and a round dozen earwigs who have been caught napping when the carriers went off and have sought refuge in the folds of my shirt and trousers. Experience has taught me that these must be shaken very carefully before putting on, otherwise when I have ridden half a mile or so I am aware of something tickling my left leg, I murmur to my messenger, the train of horses comes to a standstill, I dismount and try to capture the brute, who of course takes fright and rushes down into the laced-up portion round the calf, so that I have to retire behind a tree (fortunately we have stopped near one) and undress thoroughly. A rather difficult situation to 'carry off' without loss of dignity!

We always seemed to travel in hordes. In England, a man may try to impress his neighbours by the size of his car. In Hausa country the District Head, particularly if he were not too sure of himself, would seek to do so by the number of his retainers. Custom and courtesy required him to meet the touring officer and the Sultan's representative accompanying him when they entered his district, and often we found quite a little army awaiting us at the stream bed or clearing in the bush which marked the boundary. Here all dismounted to exchange salutations. Chief and followers were clad in voluminous gowns, embroidered with geometric patterns down the front, fringe and sleeves, topped by yards of turban, often coloured with the local indigo dye, a lot of which came off on the cheeks and beard of the wearer. Horses too had come dressed overall, with silver bridles, ornamental moon shaped stirrups and a clutter of colourful but impractical trappings and saddlery which looked

Northern Nigeria – Sokoto continued, 1937–8

as though it would break under stress, and usually did. There was the inevitable drummer and sometimes an instrumentalist as well with a long booming horn like the kind used to summon cattle from distant Alpine pastures. Brave sight and sound though it was, the show unfortunately produced the opposite effect to what was intended. 'Obviously his salary doesn't stretch to all that lot,' the touring officer was thinking to himself, with his senses always alerted to the slightest signs of maladministration. They needed to be, for the Hausa peasant, unlike the southerner, was an extremely long-suffering person, who had to be provoked beyond endurance before he would come forward with any complaint. Partly this was a matter of simple prudence, for the European was a rare and fleeting visitor while the District and Village Head were with him all his life. But another and perhaps stronger reason for their tolerance of oppression was that they expected nothing else; chiefs were chiefs and people were people, and everyone had to rest content with the life that Allah had given him.

Means of oppression were manifold, but the taxation system provided some of the easiest opportunities. First, because it was not a flat rate or poll tax as obtained almost everywhere else in Africa but a graduated tax based on income – in a country where no personal records were kept and monetary income was almost unknown, except to the tiny minority of Government and commercial employees. This rather sophisticated concept was applied in quite a simple manner. The initial step was to fix the sum of tax to be collected by each N.A., which before the days of inflation did not vary much from year to year. The total sum was then divided between districts, of which there were a score or more in the Sokoto N.A., by the Sultan and his Council, aided by the D.O.; probably too the Resident may have had a hand in it. They knew which were the wealthy districts and which were not, and had a pretty fair idea of the seasonal variables, where the crops had done well and where they had failed. Then towards the end of the rains there would be intense activity, with the Wazir and senior officers of the N.A. taking one lot of districts and the District Officer and his staff taking another (this was one of the occasions when the protocol of indirect rule had to be relaxed slightly), and 'announced' the tax to be paid in the coming year in each of them. All this had been done before my own touring began but I had been out with Backhouse on several of these tax announcing missions, concerning one of which I wrote:

> The incidence of tax, in this case about 5/6d, falls on the adult male population only. There are about five or six villages in this district, and according to their respective wealth this figure is readjusted at a preliminary meeting between the D.O. and District Head and Village Heads, so that one village which has had a prosperous year may be assessed at about 6/3d, others at 5/– or less. But the villages have not all an equal population, and the total of the incidence at different rates must still come out at 5/6d, so quite a lot of calculation has to be done. When the distribution is finished, to the satisfaction of the Village Heads, they go off in groups with the hamlet heads who have been sitting at a respectful distance, and in the case of the village which has been assessed at 5/– some of the hamlets are assessed at 5/–, others at 4/6d, and when the hamlet heads go home they will reallot the incidence of taxation per individual, according to his wealth, which of course in Africa everyone knows. Each Village Head comes up with his hamlet heads before the D.O. in turn, and if they have any grouse he may make some adjustment to the Village Head's distribution . . . We – he – started work at about 5.30 and finished after dark. Everyone is present and hears all that goes on, so as to make subsequent extortion less likely. At the end of it all, when the lamp has been lit, all are called together and given a short homily on the virtues of paying their taxes promptly.

A few weeks after this, when out on tour, I wrote again about

> watching the tax coming in and trying to increase the pace of it. The Resident started a competition a few years ago.

Northern Nigeria – Sokoto continued, 1937–8

Statements are issued to touring officers showing just how much tax has been received from each area, and armed with this you approach the D.H. and say in a meaningful sort of way "I see that Sarkin X of Y has got in half of *his* tax already". It's not quite fair, because the tax can't all be announced simultaneously, and Sarkin X may have had a week's start, but more likely your remark falls flat, because the D.H.'s ideas are so parochial that he's not the least bit interested in what other District Heads have been doing. Does this insistence on tax sound to you rather hard-hearted and mercenary? I suppose it is, but it has – in theory at least – been evenly distributed so that everyone is able to pay his share without difficulty, and it wastes a lot of time and money getting it all paid in. If you don't assist as hard as ever you can, you're just encouraging the age-old habits of the Hausa in putting off till tomorrow what he can equally well do today ... There is very little idea of thrift; his crops may do well one year but he has never been in the habit of putting things by for the morrow, which means that his standard of living will never improve. You can see him thinking – "Oh bother the government, where shall we find five shillings to give them this year?", and as often as not they have to sell a goat to do it, but nobody wants a lot of goats all at once, and so the price is much lower than what they would get at any other time.

In some districts the tax came in quickly and was all over in a matter of weeks. In others it dragged on for months. These were the areas whose District Heads were weak or unco-operative, and very often these districts had a low standard of efficiency as well. The census lists on which the division was based may have been worked out incorrectly in the first place, and the need to revise it gave a chance of manipulating the individual assessments. The victims were usually those least able to defend themselves; going through the assessment lists one was reminded of the supplication in the Litany on behalf of the 'Fatherless children and widows, and all that are desolate and oppressed'.

Colonial Postscript

Those old Church fathers had known what they were about in bracketing the first two and last groups together.

> I was checking a census list in one part of the town when I came across a widow assessed at a high rate, and being, according to the census list (which contains details of household, farms, property in the form of goats etc.) a person of very limited means. Normally women don't pay taxes at all, but occasionally they are householders and taxed in their own names, always very lightly though. However, if the District Head is corrupt they are people it may be possible to bully and assess at an extravagant amount. Thinking of this I went through the census list and examined the case of every woman who appeared there under her own name (there weren't many) and found my suspicions justified. The D.H. was a nasty bit of work, and had assessed himself very low. I had the greatest pleasure in revising the women's tax and placing the entire surplus on his own. And the poor men of the village will be equally pleased when they hear the old robber has had one in the eye!

This tax, known as *Haraji*, was paid only by the settled Hausa population. The nomad Fulani paid a different tax, known as *Jangali* which was assessed on their livestock, but the numbers were difficult to ascertain and collection often quite a problem. 'I seem to remember telling you,' I wrote,

> that I had found a difference in the books of 2000 cattle less this year than last and I had a sort of idea that if this story was true then there must be a correspondingly increased number elsewhere – not very deep so far but you just wait! – and that as the districts to which they are reported to have gone are "bush" and consequently backward, they probably hadn't been counted and hadn't paid tax. Now on the first of November they are safe, and their owners can take them up to the northern areas round Sokoto in perfect confidence, but until then it's dangerous and they have got to wait in bush . . .

Northern Nigeria – Sokoto continued, 1937–8

But now the rains are over the bush is drying up and there is hardly any water – I rode through fifteen miles of it yesterday and only passed a single pool. South of that is the river, then waterless bush for another 30 miles or so. So this is what they'll do, they'll cross the river and hide in the bush, falling back on the river every day or two. My messenger got busy making discreet enquiries in the town (that's really the chief reason for having him) and established the fact that at least some were there. Anyway I was up at 2.30 this morning, for a rendezvous in the town with the Ardo, Umaru, Dan Chimale (are they all old friends by now? – they should be) and we were miles in the bush before dawn – awful riding down forest paths with wet and dewy branches slapping into you. We separated, Dan Chimale and Ardo going east, Umaru and self west, we didn't see a thing but they rounded up a herd of 15. I was sick at not making a haul but pretty pleased there was something to substantiate my theory, on the strength of which we've worked out a terrific plan. I'm going on into Denge territory and as soon as I get there I'll see the news gets around that Sarkin Borah (of Denge) is on the look out for all cattle that haven't paid tax and try to cross into his territory before the end of the month. Ardo meanwhile stays here but keeps quiet and sits tight on the river, and nabs them when they come out to have a drink! It won't work out as nicely as that of course but we might collect a few hundred cattle taxes (1/6d per head) as a reward. Jangali is a thing about which the African D.H. becomes really enthusiastic and at the height of the season it's great sport, since you may have to ride hard for your cattle and even leap off your horse onto their owner, I am told, in the best rodeo traditions. Set a thief to catch a thief, or put the average D.H. onto a job of this kind and he'll love it – anyway no-one has ever found anything else for which he'll get up at 2.30 in the morning.

Dan Chimale was the Sultan's representative and his name recurs frequently in letters of this period. While I was reporting on him in my touring diaries, no doubt he was reporting to his own master on the newly appointed cadet. But there was no competition – quite the contrary.

The system is that one makes any remarks to the Sultan's representative, who repeats them to the District Head, who repeats them to the official responsible (indirect rule again!) so that by the time it reaches the last there's not much doubt about the meaning, and if the original remark has been in any degree forcible, it is apt to gather strength in the process.

In a country as large as Northern Nigeria any sort of rule in which an outside power was involved could not be anything but indirect, whatever the arguments might be in its favour – or against. Many districts went for years without a visit from a British touring officer and a good many of the villagers had never seen one in a lifetime. But the native courtesy and discretion of the Hausa people were such that one was never made at all conscious of their curiosity. Only in one village do I recall sitting under a tree with the local officials, idly watching the evening procession of women to the well in the middle distance and suddenly noticing that the same faces reappeared more quickly than the pots on their heads could ever have been replenished! For all that, these visits must have been tremendous events in the locality which, for twenty-four hours at least, was shaken out of the routine of centuries. One of the events which caused the greatest disturbance was the interest of the Sokoto N.A., or perhaps it would be truer to say of Backhouse its D.O., in public health. All compounds had to be swept, all the alleyways cleaned of debris, and a clear space left between the edge of the village and the standing crops around it. Often the first sight of a village was a haze of dust and smoke which lay above it, as preparations were feverishly concluded. A check on the general tidiness was the first job to be carried out on arrival, in case further efforts were required later in the day. 'There was nothing that had been dead for any length of time lying about,' was the somewhat faint praise accorded to one village, and this was a model compared to some of them. In these the whole

Northern Nigeria – Sokoto continued, 1937–8

population would be set to work to tidy it up, to everyone's discomfort – a disagreable job, but at least it would make things easier next time round, as well as in the villages still to be visited, since one's reputation tended to precede one in such matters. This was not just tidiness for its own sake, but the beginning of a programme of public health improvement in a vast area, with infinitesimal resources of men and money. There were a variety of jobs to be done on tour. 'Oh, you are going out to so-and-so?', the District Engineer might say, 'then would you look at such-and-such?', mentioning a feeder road for which a few tens of pounds had been set aside in the provincial budget. One would go there, pay some labour perhaps, and correct a line proposing to advance up an impossibly steep gradient. Or a dispensary had run out of laxatives – its most popular line in medicines – or a school out of chalk, and the teacher was waiting for further supplies to arrive this year, next year, some time, never, but doing nothing himself to hasten the process. Visiting schools was always great fun, particularly when the District Head clearly had an interest, as the visitors' book would show, recording a weekly inspection. These youngsters were the generation on whom the future of the country depended. By contrast, the Alkali's court belonged very much to the Nigeria of the present. Matrimonial cases were in the majority, some of them complicated as only such issues can be, and assault cases, in which the defendant was usually accused of knocking off the plaintiff's 'Fula' (the skullcap supporting the turban, but generally worn without it), in which a large sum of money happened to have been concealed. No sort of evidence was barred, hearsay or otherwise, but in the end adjudication relied on none of it.

'Would the plaintiff be prepared to swear to 5/–?' Awkward wriggle.

'4/–then?'

'Yes'. (He was never actually sworn.)

Listening to these cases gave one marvellous insight into the language, manner of life, ways of thought of the people, combined with considerable admiration of the judge's discernment. However, when it came to checking the court cash, which seldom tallied with the receipts, he had to admit defeat, so that we were able to part with mutual respect.

The principal character in each District, after the District Head, was the Mallam or scribe, an overworked and underpaid official with an immense responsibility not only to be honest himself but to persuade others to be honest too, if not for its own sake then because it would be in their best interests. (There was never any Hausa proverb corresponding to 'Honesty is the best policy' – the sentiment would have carried no conviction!) He was usually well-trained, and often highly intelligent. Beneath him were the Village Mallams, some of them hardly trained at all, and quite mystified as to what to do with the forms with which they were provided. With the space for the date on the tax receipt, for instance, they could get as far as the day of the week but no further. An illuminating hour or two could be spent in going through their assessments and checking the facts they recorded with the reality. 'Number of children' got mixed up with the 'Goats' column further across the page, with startling consequences. Yet it was these figures which were added together to arrive at the District total, and the District totals to form the Provincial total, and the Provincial totals to form the Nigerian total, and at that stage they would be printed, and start having a life of their own, independent of reality, providing tools for economists and ammunition for experts in the League of Nations. No connection of course with what was happening in the 'bush'. 'The word "bush" seems to need some explanation,' I wrote to my mother, and perhaps not only to her.

> 'To go to bush may mean to go out from your house, to go from Kano to Sokoto, to go from Sokoto to a lesser town, and so on down the scale, or even to hit your golf ball off the fairway, while to "go bush" is to eat your dinner in your pyjamas, or do anything else considered uncivilized.'

It was the job of the touring officer to be inquisitive, to poke his nose into everything: genealogies, water rights, where do the

Northern Nigeria – Sokoto continued, 1937–8

flies go in the winter time (an important one, that), the origins and present-day reasons for facial markings, religious beliefs, customs, the price of grain in the local markets, all was grist to his mill. 'Who are you, where are you going and what are you carrying?' Dan Chimale asked the donkey driver as our cavalcade overtook him, knowing from experience that if he did not do so he would be asked to ask him anyway. Frightened out of his wits by this entirely unexpected encounter, the donkey driver said that his name was Audu, he was travelling from the market of X to the market of Y, and the bag on his donkey's back contained salt. Good, that was all we wanted to know. An hour or so later (this is a true story) we met another donkey driver, going in the opposite direction. His name was Moman, the bag on his donkey's back contained salt, and he, by God, was travelling from the market of Y to the market of X. This story does not necessarily have any explanation than that the Hausa liked trading and found it more interesting to do so in another town. But it makes some nonsense of classical economics! Other enquiries might yield information of some importance however. In the country near Sokoto where the farms were small and the land had insufficient time to lie fallow it had become customary for quite a large number of the menfolk to go off to the south for a month or two during the dry season, where they would act as builders' labourers, cocoa farm workers or in some other job, from which they would return with money to pay their tax and a bolt or two of cloth as a present for their families. This important annual migration only came to light in the first place as a result of the curiosity of a touring officer asking questions.

But asking questions by itself was non-productive. Like the Alkali listening to the court complainants, one tended to get only the routine answer. Thus if one asked that considerable naturalist, Dan Gusau, the horse-boy walking or trotting behind the pony, 'What is that?' he would reply, in all seriousness, 'That, master, is a bird'. 'What kind of bird?' To which he would reply either that he did not know, or give the bare name, and there the conversation ended, unless by good luck some other member of the party disagreed, claiming that it was a different kind of bird, in which case a real dialogue began, beginning with birds but going on perhaps to a lot more important and interesting things which one would strain one's ears and understanding to follow, making mental notes of the unknown word or expression to be checked later, the points which might be brought up on some informal occasion.

Here is an example from another letter.

This evening I rode out to visit Surame, about two miles from here, which is a most impressive ruined city away in the bush, or seven cities to be precise, each surrounded by a prodigious battlement of stone – and you have to realize that no native building of today is made of anything but mud to see that it dates from a time when Nigeria was a very different place to what it is today. Quite what sort of place it was I got by degrees out of the mouths of Umaru, my horse-boy and one or two others in the course of the journey home, already knowing a little about it from various histories I have read, in the strangest mixture of fact and the most extraordinary stories. They abound with tales of startling deeds of cruelty and prodigality; as an example of the first I was shown the place where anyone who had vexed the chief was thrown to death from the walls, and of the second, the site of the stables which were carpeted a foot deep with sand brought on camel back from nearly a hundred miles away (the fine quality of the Azben horses from the edge of the Sahara is attributed to the fact that the sand there is soft to gallop on or lie on). Mortar for the walls was brought from 30 or 40 miles away by an endless chain of slaves passing from hand to hand, and the soil for the chief's own dwelling was also brought from miles away in what is now French territory (this lay towards the Sahara in the north). The last fact has great intrinsic probability – anthropologically it is on a par with Naaman's mule loads of earth and similar stories are to be found in most mythologies. The huge ramparts remained; of the houses, particularly those that housed the chief's wives – streets of

Northern Nigeria – Sokoto continued, 1937–8

them, it being in the pre-Mohammedan era – there was nothing left except the site, which could be traced here and there. They seemed very small, and I learned the explanation, the world is shrinking and everything shrinks with it, so that a house which measures ten feet now measured 15 feet then, in proof of which is it not a well-known fact that a journey to Sokoto which now takes three days at one time took seven? I suggested that the reason might be that roads had been opened up which made communications more rapid now, but it was not accepted and I said no more, since once you start being "all-knowing" they agree with what you say and good-bye to hearing anything else of interest. They are all very, very sensitive to an unfriendly or disbelieving atmosphere and won't air their views if there is the least danger of being laughed at.

One's great opportunity of hearing things is to get them started talking about things that interest you, only among themselves – this they were doing this evening, and though I miss a great deal of what is being said I hear something too. I've been finding out all I can lately about the dangers and powers of jujus of which there are a number of different varieties; they know and admit that Europeans are immune, but that does not make them any less real and terrible to themselves. There was a well in the city which I particularly wanted to see, and the guide knew that I knew of its existence, but he had lost it, so he said. Now Africans don't lose things to which they have been in the habit of going and I am quite sure that something had led him to think that there was danger there, and nothing would make him admit to where it was to be found. The men who built the city were of course of a size and strength far surpassing the men of today – and indeed the walls are so far beyond anything that the present day African is capable of building that it's not an unnatural supposition. You will again find the anthropological parallel in Genesis, Chap 6.

'I came across a bush doctor in a village the other day,' the same letter continues.

Colonial Postscript

The village head had had a fall and fractured his forearm, and I saw the splint the local medico had made, a very efficient affair except that it had been put on rather too tightly and the arm was not in a sling as it should have been. I called the "doctor" and had a talk with him. Like all callings, his is a strictly family affair and knowledge is handed from father to son. It would be a very good thing indeed if it were possible to give the sons some knowledge of European medicine with which to supplement their local knowledge, as they are the people to whom the native goes if he feels ill or has a sore etc., not to the European doctor, who is remote and living in an atmosphere of whitewash and antiseptics, of which they feel thoroughly frightened. There is a beautiful native hospital in Sokoto which is kept filled with prisoners, who have to go there if they are sick, and the dregs from the town – nobody of any influence or social standing would dream of going there. (It was the same with education in some places, where it was the Koranic schools in a backyard, not the new teachers, that still carried all the prestige.) My boys come to me if they have cut themselves and I give them iodine, they know it does them good, and they know me well enough not to be frightened, they also come for quinine when they have a touch of fever, but even they prefer to try their native remedies first, though they should be accustomed enough to contact with Europeans, if anyone was. Just before I left one of them came to me with his child in a most pitiable state – masses of sores for which I could do nothing, and I sent him to hospital to get properly treated. But the child had been ill for days and had been treated with a concoction from a native tree "gabaruwa", and I sent a sample of this to the hospital. I don't think they were more than politely interested.

Talking about hospitals, this may be the time for one of my favourite African stories which concerns the time, a year or so later, when the Free French troops were establishing an advance base in Maiduguri, in Borno Province, before their assault on the Fezzan, in Libya, as part of the North African campaign. It

Northern Nigeria – Sokoto continued, 1937–8

was obvious to all concerned that the amenities which had previously existed in this sleepy little town with a handful of British, government or commercial people, would not be enough for the French soldiers, and that something would have to be done about it. So the Resident called on the Shehu who said certainly, he understood just what was required, and would arrange for half a dozen suitable young ladies to call at the District Office on the morrow. Which they did, and were sent up to the hospital by the D.O., but his note to the doctor in charge went astray, or they went in by the wrong door, and all six of them were vaccinated!

One of the points which emerges from this narrative is, I hope, the gap that existed between ourselves, the small band of European administrators, and the native peoples of Northern Nigeria. We lived totally apart in our separate communities, we dressed differently and ate differently, we had different standards, beliefs, views about the meaning of life and the part that the individual had to play in it. It could be said with truth that we encouraged these differences, that we preferred to speak to the Africans in Hausa because we did not want them to speak English to us, and were immediately suspicious of the motives of any African who attempted to adopt European ways and patterns of behaviour. No doubt we did so subconsciously in order to preserve the legend of European supremacy, already being undermined every time a new road or school was opened, and soon to be finally destroyed by the consequences of a European war. But it should not therefore be concluded that the theory of indirect rule was so much humbug. Apart from its practical advantages, the institutions which had been allowed to remain when the country was conquered had already adapted themselves quite out of recognition and could be expected to go on doing so up to and beyond eventual independence. In the meanwhile the people would not be left, as had so often tragically happened elsewhere, without faith in the old regime and without confidence in the new. Another point which may have shown up equally clearly is that the wide gap between European and African could be bridged by mutual respect and

Colonial Postscript

understanding. Touring helped this greatly, as travelling together and sharing the minor hardships which inevitably occur on journeys brought them closer together.

The people one got to know best outside one's immediate entourage were the District Heads, of whom there are a number of thumbnail sketches in my letters but unfortunately nothing complete. Sarkin Adar of Kworre, 'the type of man who would be happiest sitting at home with his feet on the mantlepiece, chewing kola-nut; successive A.D.O.s have forced him into activity which he does not like'. Sarkin Ardo of Shuni (the cow-catcher)

> looked very doleful when I first saw him this morning and I excused his presence as he has got dysentry. I wasn't surprised when I saw the water in my bath this evening, it had so much foreign matter in suspense that any part of the body underneath it was completely hidden.

I suggested that the Geological Department paid him a visit and sank a tube-well. The titles were hereditary like the office itself tended to be, and often bore no relation to the locality; thus the Sarkin Katsina had his bestowed on him when sent off to conquer Katsina, which he had failed to do but his successors kept the title. The D.H. Sifawa was 'rather a swollen-headed individual'. But one had to be careful. 'It is so easy to drop the most dreadful bricks when going to a new district,' I wrote,

> for instance I was speaking to a D.H. in rather strong terms, hinting in fact that he would be reported to the Sarkin Mussulmi (the Sultan), only to find out later that the S.M. was his brother, by a different wife of his father's, which is a complicating factor that doesn't have to be reckoned with in even the most abstruse family tree at home.

The one who made the biggest impression was the District Head of Raba, a young man, well educated and

Northern Nigeria – Sokoto continued, 1937–8

full of energy and ideas and, I suspect, much better qualified to speak to me in English than I to him in Hausa. I tried not to let my mouth hang open while listening to him addressing his people on anti-Guinea worm measures – it's something so far beyond the stage that most District Heads have arrived at, but I suppose as the old type die off there will be more and more of the new school of thought. I hope they'll all manage the difficult compromise as well as he has done.

Unlike all the other District Heads I had come across, Sarkin Raba greeted me with a handshake, and sat beside me on a chair, instead of on a mat on the ground, as we talked to his people. All these details went down into the touring diary, which was read by Backhouse and then by Carrow, who questioned me closely about the man on my return. Many years later I met him again in the house of an M.P. in London, speaking excellent English and very self-assured, which was hardly surprising as in the meantime he had become the Northern Premier. This was the Sardauna of Sokoto whose brutal murder by an Ibo officer soon afterwards was to make the Nigerian civil war inevitable.

Because this aristocracy (which is what it was; no man of humble origin could hope to become a chief) failed at times to reach our standards it does not follow that they fell short of their own. Their forefathers had won the authority they now exercised, and this was unquestioned either by the people or by themselves. They knew they were different and indeed they were different. I recall the conferences in the resthouse when plans for the following day were being discussed. When a point had to be emphasised there was a characteristic lifting of the sleeve of the robe and a finger, not black but brown, not broad like a negro's but with the thin bone structure of the Fulani, made an elegant stroke in the sand. They had no doubts about themselves. And they had, in real and stark terms, a capacity to govern which was woefully lacking in many other people of Africa (President Kwame Nkrumah being a good example). Some months later when I was back in the Provincial Office word came to the club where we were playing tennis in the

Colonial Postscript

afternoon that there had been an uprising of sorts at Talata Mafara, down the road to the south. The D.O. and A.D.O. Sokoto left immediately, first to mobilize the N.A. police and organize transport for them, and then set off themselves. But the Wazirin Sokoto was far in advance of them. He had set out at once with a single attendant in his own car, and when he arrived in the market place of the little town thronged with spearmen and bowmen, got out of it and managed to keep them talking for hours until reinforcements arrived. You do not learn this sort of thing out of manuals of administration.

Of the Hausa people as a whole it is more difficult to make an assessment. Heussler speaks in his book, mentioned in the preceeding chapter, of 'the sacred North, a land apart, suspended in space and time . . .', according to its denigrators, 'an exotic backwater, attractive to its British protectors but administratively ineffective, corrupt and insensitive'. The relationship of some villagers to their chief was 'not unlike that of French serfs to feudal overlords in the Middle Ages'. These harsh judgements may be true but they can also be thoroughly misleading unless one remembers also the practical limitations to the speed at which political evolution can take place – one generation has to pass on before the next one can succeed it. In my recollection the 'feel' of the country and its people was altogether different from that expressed above. Perhaps one came closest to the truth after the day's work was done, when one would pick up one's gun and go off to the bush to find a guinea fowl, or after duck – thousands upon thousands of them – wheeling above the marshes in the river valleys. Some local hunter would be my companion, and always amazed me by his skill in bushcraft. This was more than mere knowledge of natural laws, it was rather that the Hausa peasant saw himself as part of nature, not superior to it as we like to suppose ourselves. In their folklore the spider, the hare, the lion and man meet one another on equal terms. I need not elaborate the point, but anyone who cares to think about it will realize without more explanation the gulf that lay between the British expatriate and the local African in their ways of thought. And he will realize

Northern Nigeria – Sokoto continued, 1937–8

too why it was that we tried so hard to cross that gulf back to them, and see the world as we had never seen it before, through eyes like theirs.

The Hausa, for their part, realized that we were not, or thought ourselves not to be, subject to the rules of their world (I mentioned this earlier in regard to juju) and had a trust in our powers almost like that which would be given to a higher being. Here is the appropriate story with which to illustrate this, and to end the chapter. It was told to me by a senior D.O. about his early days, when the machinery of government was still rudimentary. He had been trying a case in a pagan area, where the native courts if they existed at the time had only limited powers, had sentenced the man to death and now had to see that the hanging was carried out. The prisoner was perfectly composed, he accepted the fact that he had to die but when (as apparently happens on these occasions) he was blindfolded, he became suddenly frightened. 'Bature,' (Master) he called out. 'Ina nan,' (I am here) said the D.O., and the prisoner's tension relaxed. The white man was present, so all must be well.

IV
Northern Nigeria – Sokoto concluded, 1937–8

At breakfast one day half-way through November the salt suddenly started to pour freely through the hole in the saltcellar. This was the first sign that the wind had shifted to the north, and soon the Harmattan was blowing unmistakably. This was a dust-laden, drying wind not altogether pleasant but most invigorating. It turned cold, so that even two blankets were not enough for the European sleeping out under the stars, while the Africans lit fires in their huts, barricaded the doors and windows and shivered when they emerged in the mornings. But the one who really enjoyed it most was Benjie, the pony I had bought from a Frontier Force officer because he had found him no good for polo, but who had been gathering strength and stamina during our long rides through the bush and was now bursting with health and energy.

In those days Sokoto Province had few roads, and horses, which could go anywhere and even swim the rivers with their riders, provided the only means of getting about. We called them horses but they were really only large ponies, with a fair amount of the Arab in their ancestry. They had narrow hindquarters but were powerfully built in the chest and shoulders, so that they were able to move quickly in the sandy soil. For the most part only stallions were used for riding, and none of them was ever shod. The native horsemanship was different from ours; they bounced up and down in the saddle while the horse used a gait known I believe as 'tripling'. The

Northern Nigeria – Sokoto concluded, 1937–8

first thing therefore one had to do after buying a new pony was to teach him to trot, so that one could rise in the saddle in the approved riding school manner, probably a more tiring method in the long run for both horse and rider but that is the way it was. All the best horses came from French territory and usually arrived in poor condition, underfed and with saddle sores that sometimes took long to heal, but as against that they did not cost much either. They were never turned loose, but were hobbled and tied to a post in the compound where they saw all that went on around them and were regarded almost as one of the family. Benjie was 'the only one who understands English,' I said in one of my letters. Benjie was the first and best of a number of ponies, he was followed by Buzu, so called because of his decidedly Roman nose, Billie, who taught me how to play polo, and Beltane, a large black creature who promised well but unfortunately succumbed to some equine disease which was never precisely identified. Benjie's qualities only became apparent after I had returned from my first spell of touring and tried him against other ponies in the station. He performed so well that I decided to enter him for an Easter race meeting at Zaria, some 250 miles away to the south. Dan Gusau set off with him two or three weeks beforehand. I saw him off and

> could not but admire the small preparations he had to make for the journey – a bag with halter and hobbling ropes, a curry comb and some soap (for the horse), the money I had given him and the rather exiguous clothes he stood up in were all he wanted. And we can't move a mile without a dozen porters or so!

Another preparation Dan Gusau had made but didn't tell me about until afterwards was to buy an amulet, no doubt a small purse of leather with a verse from the Koran sewn into it, which he wove into the hairs of Benjie's tail. With this done he set off full of hope and in high spirits. 'Benjie has arrived safely in Zaria,' I wrote three weeks later, he was evidently in good form and spent the first night knocking down the walls of his stable, as he had taken a dislike to the horse next door. Tom Slator is looking after him and tried him out over the track. He did not like the shortness of it and was a devil to stop. Don't I know!

Carrow went off on tour after Easter so I was able to get away too and took the road south in a borrowed car 'piled high with my boy, my bed, a kettle, some food and a couple of tins of petrol'. Zaria was 'so lovely, with large comfortable houses, and so green. It got greener and greener all the way down and I might have come to a different country altogether'. It was fun to meet Tom and other old Cambridge friends after keeping one's own up with senior D.O.s in the north. But all this was incidental to the main purpose of the visit, thus described in the following weekly letter:

Benjie was entered for three races – Novices' Sprint (3 furlongs), the Maiden Four (4 furlongs) and the Owners' Race (5 furlongs). He won the second, easily, from a field of seventeen runners, and got second place in the first and third. He would have won these easily but for trouble at the starting gate which sent him off two or three lengths behind the rest (in the third at the critical moment we were facing the wrong direction!). I don't remember very much about it, as I was so frightfully excited and, in the case of the third race, in a cold sweat for several hours before it. In fact I sweated so much, and had been doing so for the previous two or three days, that I weighed in for the last race, carrying a racing saddle at 12 stone 6lb, and had to put a pound weight in my pocket to make weight. Everyone was talking about Benjie and said he was one of the best horses that had come out of the north for many years. He was in splendid condition and looked marvellous. Speer rode him well and I sold Benjie to him at the end for much less than I should have done, (but still four times as much as I had paid for him) as there were people who would have gone up to £50 for him. Still, I made £6 on the tote, and £15 in prize money, plus

Northern Nigeria – Sokoto concluded, 1937–8

some plate which I will be sending to you soon, and so even if I did spend a good deal on champagne I was well able to afford it! I was very sad saying goodbye to him but it would have been no good bringing him back up here and trekking him round bush places until I had spoiled the speed that was in him. Sokoto is a good place to buy horses but it's no place to make the best use of them. You and Dad must get the port out tonight and drink to blue, white crossbands and black cap, my (borrowed) racing colours, for it's the biggest success I've ever had and I'm not likely to pick a winner like that for many years to come.

So ended the account of a memorable occasion without any mention of the real hero of the day, Dan Gusau, who was suitably rewarded and arrived back in Sokoto dressed for the first time in robe and turban, for he was from now on the prince of horseboys in our little community and assumed a gravity suited to the new position.

The Harmattan blew with great vigour that year and Christmas had been really cold, so that we were able to enjoy sitting round the fire at one of Sokoto's famous parties where one would start having dinner about ten o'clock or half past, finish near midnight and go on talking or playing party games into the small hours. Carrow had been a renowned party-goer in his time but having recently acquired a wife in his middle age was now a reformed character, though there were still occasional glimpses of the old ways. 'We had a colossal dinner party at the Residency,' I wrote of one weekend when a party of French officers from over the border came to enjoy our hospitality,

> with speeches galore; the French D.O. made no less than six and rode the Resident's horse round the table in the course of the meal. There was a rumour that Germany had crossed the Czech frontier and inevitably a great deal of talk about *l'entente cordiale* and the next war.

Having returned to headquarters and learnt enough Hausa while on tour to pass the first language exam I had to settle

Colonial Postscript

down for a long spell in the Provincial Office. 'The work there is not really very difficult, it needs experience and a lot of care rather than any high degree of intelligence,' I wrote.

> It is a clearing house for multitudes of files which keep on coming up to be dealt with, and the person in charge does not have to take much action himself, but must know the right person to pass the file to. Difficult subjects are passed round a lot, as officers try to get rid of them onto someone else, a sport known as "passing the baby" in official circles and "red tape" by the outside world.

The worst of them were the Treasury Queries – queries raised by one of the Accountant General's clerks months after the event about some payment which did not appear to have been properly authorized or was not in accordance with Nigerian General Orders. As often as not the officer concerned had been posted to another Province or had gone on leave, but wherever he might be the Query pursued him relentlessly, as explanation was followed by counter-argument and argument by further clarification, all about a shilling or two. 'Apart from the Treasury stuff,' I wrote,

> which I ought to check up, as I'm financially responsible, but haven't time to, I find myself sending in returns of Births and Deaths, Capital Sentences (referred to as 'executions'), reports on Boards of Survey, Wells, Forests, Cattle Diseases, Groundnuts etc. A lot of the returns are nil, many more are imaginary and still more are only "founded" on fact – there is no machinery for collecting many kinds of statistics, so the person in charge of the Division just has to guess. Headquarters (by which I meant the Secretariat at Kaduna, for which we had the usual out-station contempt) have an ever-growing appetite for them and yet if they are so unreliable I can't see their usefulness. We were asked the other day what we thought of a return of road accidents, the matter was put to Divisions in the usual way and the D.O. Argungu reported

Northern Nigeria – Sokoto concluded, 1937–8

cheerfully that there was only one car in the Division, his own, so he would obviously have first hand information about any accidents!

Among the circulars coming through the office were the monthly 'Jeddah reports'. The reason why these were copied to Northern Territory Residents went quite a long way back into history – to the Mahdi rebellion in the Sudan in 1881, the Mad Mullah in Somaliland in the early years of the century and, more recently, the attempt to proclaim a 'jihad' or holy war in the Middle East between 1914–18. The possibility that there might one day be a revival of fanaticism of this sort was never far from the minds of the British administrators, particularly in a country like Northern Nigeria with a large Mohammedan population whose most famous historical figure, now revered as a saint, had begun his career by raising the standard of revolt against the then rulers of the country in the name of religion. This concern for popular opinion was shown in a number of ways, in the quite severe restrictions placed on any attempt by Christian missionaries to win converts among the Moslem population, in the rigid control over the sale of liquor (which was one of my jobs in the Provincial Office), and in the arrangements of the annual pilgrimage to Mecca. Quite large numbers of the population in the north made the pilgrimage once in a lifetime and there was a special scheme for providing the more wealthy among them with passports and the golden sovereigns which they would require for entry into the Holy Cities. But this was no help to the poor, who had to spend months and very often years slogging it on foot across Africa, earning money as they went. In Mecca they would meet other pilgrims from all parts of the world and it was obviously interesting and might be important for us to know what sort of influences they might be subject to when they got there. It was the function of the British Ambassador in Jeddah to supply this intelligence, and copies of his despatches came to us regularly.

I can still see these documents headed, 'To Viscount Halifax, Secretary of State for Foreign Affairs – Sir – I have the honour to report . . .', and imagine as I did then, their unknown author settling down to write in the sweltering heat of this comfortless Red Sea port and, at the other end, their distinguished recipient in Whitehall commanding his Personal Secretary to make sure that, whatever might happen to the despatches from Berlin, Paris or Vienna, the Jeddah report was to be laid before him the moment it arrived. For this was a report with a difference, full of sound observation but also gay, amusing, and with an eye for a good story! Some of these stick in my memory even today.

There was another case of stealing in the *suq* (market) today, the offender being punished according to Shari'a law by having his right hand cut off. It is said that if similar treatment were accorded to the Ministers in His Majesty's treasury, there would be nothing left of them but their navels.

Or again, 'His Highness (this would be the son of the first King Ibn Saud) has just returned from a visit to Europe, owing a debt of £400 to Messrs Gellatly Hankey, for a set of distorting mirrors which caught His Highness's fancy'. One can imagine what joy they must have created among the wives imprisoned in the Harem! (Many years later, I discovered that the author must have been Sir Reader Bullard, formerly of the Levant Consular Service, whose reports, according to his obituary in *The Times*, 'were eagerly looked forward to and had a wide circle of readers outside the department to which they were addressed' – including a remote Provincial Office in Northern Nigeria!)

As is often the case, intense superstition and deep religious feeling existed quite happily side by side. The Hausa people had great faith in the efficacy of charms, as is shown by Dan Gusau's preparations for the race meeting which I have already described. Another example of it occurred in the Resident's own household while I was working at the Provincial Office. Mrs Carrow had had 'words' with one of the servants who, feeling that his job was in danger, had consulted a local medicine man and bought from him a potion for arousing sympathy in the heart of the person who drank it. With this he doctored one of

Northern Nigeria – Sokoto concluded, 1937–8

the bowls of soup on the way from the kitchen to the dining room, but at some point they got mixed up, just as would have happened in an Elizabethan romance, and the bowl containing the love philtre got placed in front of the Resident. Carrow took but one sip, and immediately summond the cook, who produced what was left of the soup in the pan, when of course the whole story came out. To make a really effective charm, it was necessary to procure something which had been in close contact with the person on whom it was to be used, and for this reason my own boys were always most careful to sweep up and bury out of sight any hair clippings left after the barber had paid a visit. Once I asked the head boy why he did this, and got the fatuous answer I deserved, as he would never have admitted what was the real reason.

Belief in an unseen world about them predisposed the Hausa towards religion in the more formal sense, and Mohammedanism was a dominating influence in the life of a society which, at that time, was still barely touched by European ideas. They turned naturally towards Mecca, and in the most literal sense. Every Hausa man seemed to have an inbuilt compass, so that one would say to another: 'Pick it up by the north end', even when speaking of some object in an enclosed room. This was not altogether surprising in a country where a sizeable part of the population turned to the east in prayer five times a day. One of the attractions of the Moslem faith to its African adherents was the sense it gave them of belonging to a wider brotherhood in which there were no distinctions of class or colour. But to a people so hedged in by the mysteries of their own imagination as the Hausa it must have had an additional appeal; they gained a feeling of security through carefully observing its established rituals even if they did not fully comprehend them.

The rituals were demanding, which made them the more popular – just as medicine is deemed more effective when it has an unpleasant taste! Once again, as in Aden, the fortitude demanded in carrying out the month-long fast made a deep impression on me. Another attractive aspect of Islam was its total divorce from materialism. A 'mosque' was any space by the roadside, provided it was clean. The idea of special vestments would have been unthinkable, and so would the idea of prayer without having performed the ablutions. At the great feast at the end of the fast everyone wore a new robe for the occasion, but the 'mosque' was still the open hillside outside the walls of the city whose site had been chosen by the Sultan's illustrious ancestor 'because he thought that corrupting wealth would never come to such a bare and stony plateau'. This incidentally was the one time in the year when the Sultan appeared on horseback surrounded by his personal bodyguard of attendants wearing chain mail, said to date from Saracen times, to lead his people in their communal act of prayer.

Soon after Christmas we received from the south a consignment of *anini* which were the smallest coin, valued at one-tenth of a penny, with a hole through the centre and usually carried on a piece of string. Their arrival was supposed to herald a time of dearth and it was true that prices had dropped alarmingly, a ton of groundnuts being sold for only £4/12/6d compared with £7/13/– the previous season. There were other signs and portents, chiefly connected with the weather, and I noted at the time considerable 'agitation' on this account and general agreement that 1938 was going to be a bad year. In the middle of February it began to be really hot, with temperatures around 115°F, dry heat like an oven door being opened. Then in March, when the country was at its barest and all burned up, the trees started putting on leaves. I was out one evening, having bicycled over to a friend's bungalow on some business connected with the club accounts. The night was still and in the middle of our work I walked over to the verandah, summoned there by a mysterious, powerful scent such as I had never met before – what could it be? 'That is wet Africa,' said the old coaster, matching the mood of the moment, and that is what it was. The long drought had broken and the first rains were falling, hundreds of miles away as it turned out, for our own did not arrive for another two or three months, but there was no doubt they were on their way.

By this time I had moved from my 'bush' house to one which

Northern Nigeria – Sokoto concluded, 1937–8

was 'semi-bush', meaning it had started to be built as a permanent bungalow but was not completed before funds ran out. It was just across the road from the Provincial Office, most conveniently, as the work there was heavy and mails or telegrams often arrived at unforeseen hours. During this period the 'small boy' left and I acquired a new servant, this time a Fulani. This was most unusual; most of the Fulani youths one came across unexpectedly in the bush, standing on one leg, staff in hand, Phrygian cap on head, gazing with fierce possessiveness at their cattle grazing in the middle distance, and hardly less wild than they were. They were not often tamed and, if my Dan Fulani was a fair specimen, this was no great loss so far as domestic service was concerned. But he was an engaging character, free from any of the humility which marked the Hausa, unbelievably simple. Had I remained longer in this country, I would have tried to get to know the Fulani and learn their language. 'I was asking Dan Fulani about the ages of man,' I wrote,

> when a person ceases to be a "boy" and becomes "grown up", and begins to be "old" (there are words in Hausa for these stages but they are not quite equivalent with the translation). We didn't get very far, because I found that he couldn't get any further than 30. He knew the word for "40", but it had no meaning for him. He could understand "30 and 10" as a whole number and, with difficulty, "30 and 20"; when I emptied a fairly full box of matches on the ground and told him to count how many there were he produced two separate piles of 20, and a third pile of seven. I failed, after trying quite hard, to get him to "realize" numbers any higher than that, and all I could achieve was a sort of admiration on his part for such wonderful mathematical skill (mine) with the implication that after all this it was hardly surprising that a person so gifted as myself could sit and work things out in an office. Never has any reputation for "brains" I may ever have acquired rested on such slight foundations, I thought! It's odd to think of 60 being commonly conceived as three

sets of 20. And the smaller numbers are, the more easily they can manage them, for instance 1/10½d is invariably 2/– less 1½d, which causes quite a lot of juggling if one who is not accustomed to think that way – as we are not – has to resolve them rapidly. You know the current and very imprecise phrase "the native mind". It means a lot of philosophical and religious conceptions which are foreign to us but even more an infinity of small differences in the way of thinking.

One day I told Dan Fulani he was going to see something surprising and put some fruit salts in a glass of water; he could hardly believe his eyes when the mixture effervesced to the rim of the glass. But to me the powers he possessed and took for granted were no less miraculous. When playing golf I never bothered to look for balls which went to 'bush' as he could always find them. 'The twelfth hole goes over a long stretch of hard beaten earth which used to be the RWAFF parade ground,' I wrote 'and he showed me where the ball had bounced – it took a fragment off the surface about the size of half a threepenny bit and was one among any number of such marks made by hooves and nailed shoes but he was perfectly sure he was right.'

The work in the Provincial Office was hard even if a fairly experienced person was doing it, and it was generally agreed that a six months stretch was quite long enough. 'My six months are up,' I wrote at the beginning of June,

> and I found the D.O. very sympathetic towards my hopes of getting away from it. I had hardly hoped to go away to what is the best touring job in the Province, that of A.D.O. in the Gwandu Division, but Michie is due for local leave and much to my surprise I am to replace him. I shall now be under Capt. Douglas in Gwandu Division away to the west and will be touring practically continuously over a very wide area from Birnin Kebbi, which will be my headquarters, down to Zuru, to Yelwa and Illo west of the Niger. There are four independent N.A.s, Zuru which is a pagan and backward area with a "third class" Chief and Council, Yauri with a "second class"

Northern Nigeria – Sokoto concluded, 1937–8

Emir at Yelwa, Illo another comic pagan chieftainship, "third class", and Gwandu a "first class" Mohammedan Emirate at Birnin Kebbi. I shall be very much on my own and able to do a lot without having to ask permission (as one can't if one's next in command is several hundred miles away and the road is washed out!). Carrow was going to make me a magistrate I think but in putting up the relevant files I found that the appointment of a cadet to this position would only be approved in very exceptional circumstances, so I don't suppose he will try ... My small boy who is a Fulani comes from round Birnin Kebbi. I asked him, if you were given the choice, what town in the world would you like best to go to? He said "well of course there *is* one simply *marvellous* place flowing with milk and honey and all that (this is a rough translation) but of course I know that I'm never likely to see it again". I said "You don't mean that one-horse town Birnin Kebbi by any chance, do you?" Of course he did, and practically fell on my neck when I told him that we would be going there in a week or two.

Carrow was not the man to be deterred from having me made a magistrate when he had made up his mind, whatever Nigerian regulations might say, and soon afterwards my appointment was gazetted. But before we left an event occurred which, the locals said, had been presaged by the signs and omens earlier in the year. 'We had a terrific storm of wind and rain on the last night of May,' I wrote, trying evidently to catch the drama of the occasion,

> and at nine o'clock the same evening Hasan, Sarkin Mussulmi, Sultan of Sokoto, joined his forefathers. He hadn't been in the best of health for some considerable time but his death was completely unexpected and took everyone by surprise. He is, as I've told you before, one of the three religious leaders in the African Moslem world, the other two being the Aga Khan and the Sultan of Morocco, and he had a great and well-deserved reputation for religious orthodoxy. He had been a

Colonial Postscript

great friend of the English ever since the early days of our coming to this country and stood by us loyally on one very critical occasion. He was much beloved by his people and it was very impressive to see the respect in which he was held by them.

The electoral council of the eight or nine flagbearers, or Shehu – or rather their descendants – were deep in council for three days and finally narrowed their choice to two and ultimately to one. This was Abubakr, the former Sardauna, his place being taken by the other candidate, the young District Head of Raba whose performance had so impressed me. The ceremony of appointment was the subject of my last letter from Sokoto and a quotation from it may fittingly end this chapter.

The ceremony took place outside the Residency and was most impressive; all the District Heads were present and most of the inhabitants of Sokoto. The Resident made a very effective speech in Hausa to the Council and the Sultan-elect and handed him over his sword and staff of office. The Alkali produced a venerable looking Koran from a moth-eaten bag and the new Sultan swore the oath of loyalty. I was acutely conscious all the time that the Union Jack floating overhead on the Residential flagstaff was very very old, and wished I had remembered to put a new one there before we started. It was rather fun too trying to spot how many District Head faces I could remember, but I found it difficult at the range they were sitting to be certain of more than one or two out of the number I had met touring last autumn.

All except the new Sultan were gorgeously dressed. His gown and turban were badly in need of a wash and had a most shabby appearance. It was interesting to discover the reason for this, partly the idea of "Whoever will be chief among you, let him be your servant", but there is more to it than that. His status, or that of anyone with servants in this country, is judged from the clothes he gives them, and not from what he is wearing himself. That is particularly true of a

Northern Nigeria – Sokoto concluded, 1937–8

Sarkin Mussulmi who can dress himself in rags and yet because he *is* the S.M. is far beyond the range of criticism, but it's equally true of myself for instance and my boys and it is a thing which many a person who has spent many years in this country has never learnt, assuming that our ideas and those of the Hausa are the same in this matter, when they are really so different . . . We hit on a happy phrase when we described chiefs as Native Authorities; they are what kings only ceased to be during the XVth century, they are the law and when there is no chief there is no law in the land (in medieval Europe a judge's authority lapsed automatically when there was no king, and they had to be reappointed when a successor was found). Traditions die hard, and when there was no Sultan the big Thursday market in the town was not attended, though there was perfect law and order it was not so in the old days when every local district head would have been supreme in his own territory, which would have made travelling very unsafe. So there was no drumming in the town (till Friday night), no marriages and no law suits, because there was no law. So everyone rich and poor was very glad when a successor was appointed, irrespective of who he might be, any Sultan being better than none. The Hausa tells you that he has great *murna*, gladness when he has a Sultan again, and has clearly felt very lost while there wasn't one. The real reason why is fascinatingly interesting when you have found it out, but not at all what you would guess without asking, I think.

V
Northern Nigeria – Zuru & Yauri, 1938–9

We spent just long enough in Birnin Kebbi for me to read the files on the Zuru and Yauri N.A.s and then plunged southwards, first by lorry and then transferring the loads to carriers. 'This country is the most complete change from Sokoto,' I wrote on the first day out,

> it is very hilly and seldom possible to gallop or even trot the ponies who have to scramble up and down steep rocky paths. The going was so difficult today that I inspected their feet as soon as I got in and was relieved to find that neither had suffered any damage. Buzu surges up and down at great speed and takes less care about placing his feet than any pony I have ridden; if there is a hole or loose boulder he is certain to put his hoof right on top of it, however he never stumbles, so I have given up trying to help him with the reins.

There was an abundance of game in the area, several varieties of buck which I saw, and leopard and lion which I did not; only the carriers in the course of an early morning march had an encounter with one, who looked at them with great eyes 'like the headlamps of a motor car', as the cook described it, before ambling off into the bush.

'There are so many Hausa settlements here,' the letter continues,

> that the pagan Dakkakari, who are a very different type to the Hausa, shorter and much broader, have lost many of their

pagan characteristics, the one which would strike you most being their complete lack of clothing. Further east we shall find them naked and unashamed (I remember Dad saying that he hoped that the natives in the part of Africa to which I was going would be properly dressed – I am afraid his hopes will be fulfilled no longer!). They drink beer too, and altogether are people whom the somewhat priggish Hausa rather despises. But as they are as good fighting material as any to be found in Nigeria (so the RWAFF say) his contempt is not displayed too obviously.

The Dakkakari did not in fact go completely naked but only nearly so. The men wore small leather aprons for the most part, the women a bunch of leaves fore and aft tied with a cord. It has to be added that they were dumpy and unprepossessing, their 'bustles' making them look faintly ridiculous and a bit like ostriches as they moved about the landscape.

The Zuru N.A. was a backwater but had at one time had its own military garrison, with two or three white officers, a European doctor, a D.O. and an A.D.O. Nearly all this past splendour had now disappeared, except for a magnificent bush house, which I shall be coming to presently. The reason for this decay was partly the building of the railway, which had rerouted traffic to the north, and partly the fact that the Dakkakari tribesmen had taken to joining the Frontier Force themselves instead of as in former times requiring a military detachment in their midst to keep them in order. So by this time the establishment was reduced to one touring officer, nominally dependent on Birnin Kebbi but in reality free to wander much as he wished, since there was no telephone, no telegraph and, as soon as the rains came, no road either. It took at least a week to get a reply to a letter, transported by runner through the bush, apart from the fact that one could be – and nearly always was – out of the station when it arrived.

Almost every one of the letters during the next six months is headed from a different village, and one of them explains why.

Colonial Postscript

In Africa one of the big difficulties about touring any large area and particularly one where there is nothing faster than a horse is the necessity of being in several places at once. Continually being on the move is a semi-solution but there are other recognized ruses which help. One sends a message to a different village telling the headman to sweep out the resthouse and bring wood or water or, where there is no resthouse, to evict a family out of one of the compounds in the village. News travels around fast and tax which has been coming in slowly suddenly puts on a spurt. A ruse like that saves a great deal of time and trouble, since if one had gone there most of the reasons for going would have been eliminated before one arrived as the threat is enough. In connection with *Jangali* (cattle tax) the threat of forcible collection is much more effective than the reality. I have come out here and the Fulani think I am going to descend on them in the early hours of the morning whereas if I was to do so I know I would find very little and probably put back the rate of collection by several weeks. There are other resources; one can send a couple of *yan doka* (N.A. police) out to a district headquarters, telling them to wait there until they get further instructions. They don't know why they have been sent, nor does the District Head, nor for that matter do I, but the D.H. is conscience-stricken and begins to look to those things which he has not done but he ought to have done.

However, it was necessary to work hard to sustain the illusion.

I wish you could have seen me at one place I stopped. It was about 5.30 in the evening, raining cats and dogs outside, my bed was in the middle of the hut and my chair parked alongside it, the bath was beside the chair and the rest of the loads on the other side of the bed, one boy squatting in each doorway out of the rain. I thought – Thank Heaven I haven't got a wife too – where would she sit!

Northern Nigeria – Zuru & Yauri, 1938–9

The house at Zuru – though I didn't spend much time there – was high and spacious, with a wide spanning grass roof 'through which the rain drips, in one place, to form a little pool on the floor'. It was here that I held my first P.I. (Prelminary Investigation) in a case which lay outside the competence of the native court.

> There were eleven witnesses, and the pagans swore that their fetish would gobble them up if they told a lie, and stepped four times over an arrow laid on the floor, "duly affirmed on an arrow", the minutes record. I was able to get all but two of them to give their evidence in Hausa, took it down in English and re-translated it back into Hausa for them to confirm. I am fairly certain that it was not Murder but Manslaughter, however I was only there to take the depositions and not to try the case so I haven't got to say. The accused had unfortunately got hold of a lie which to my great regret he produced as his own deposition but this morning after the investigation was finished he sent to say that he had another statement to make and poured out what I think was the truth.

On this second occasion

> a thunderstorm produced some marvellous noises off; I wanted to say "there's your fetish coming to gobble you up", but felt that would be using my position unfairly. Sarkin Dabai was sitting over the spot where the rain comes in and I was watching out of the corner of my eye to see just how long it would be before he moved. The majesty of the law has as you see its lighter moments.

The Dakkakari villages were partially abandoned for most of the year. They were situated on a rock or some other defensible position while the inhabitants dispersed to other huts over a wide area of bush, which they farmed in a reprehensibly improvident manner. They came back to the village for social

Colonial Postscript

events, and after the harvest, and it was the centre of their fetish-worship. Staying in one of these villages I left behind my shaving mirror. The District Head – whose village it was – made a proclamation, several in fact, and failed to recover it, until at last he took a present to the juju priest who announced that whoever had taken it would be dead the next day if it was still in his possession. It was returned during the night!

About this time the Munich crisis occurred and a message arrived from the D.O. to go down to Yelwa in Yauri Emirate where there was a telegraph office and I could be contacted in an emergency. By this time all but £50 of the *Jangali* had been gathered in, which was quite a triumph, as the market for cattle had dropped away altogether, and we were well ahead with the General Tax. So it was time for a move, and there was also another reason. One of the boys had been to me and told me that the other one, whose job it was to wash the clothes, was a leper. He indignantly denied it of course, but the fact was that he had a scar and although this did not respond to the rule of thumb test (alternate jabs with the blunt and sharp ends of a pin – the real leper cannot tell the difference) and although leprosy is not particularly contagious, it would be a relief to obtain a proper diagnosis, as there was a better chance of doing in Yelwa. It was an exhausting ride down to the great river of Nigeria, travelling always being worst in the intensely hot period immediately after the end of the rains, but we were much sustained during these three or four days by the thought of the fish we were going to eat when we got there. On the way we passed through the territory of the Gungawa, about whom there was the following review of a court case by a former Resident in the District Notebook – regrettably I had no time to follow it up with any researches of my own. 'Suit No. 2 gives a most important decision,' the extract read.

> Here the Emir (of Yauri) held that among the Gungawa pagans there could be neither adultery, bigamy or divorce. The reason given for his decision was that there was no such institution as marriage. I made enquiries in the Gungawa

Northern Nigeria – Zuru & Yauri, 1938–9

District and examined the District Court records carefully and concluded that the Emir's decision was correct. No breaches of the peace seem to arise from this curious state of affairs and consequently there would seem to be no point in objecting to it.

The authentic voice of Queen Victoria! Further south we encountered an allied tribe, the Kambarawa,

> a most curiously attired folk who wear very little except ornaments, the most striking of which are tube-shaped pieces of wood four or five inches long which hang almost horizontally from the lobes of their ears and are painted bright red at the end, also small pink and blue horns from the nostrils and lower lips. Arms and legs have white metal or brass bangles. My boys are as usual much amused and giggle as they would at a giraffe or other unlikely animal at the zoo, though not openly since I lectured them on good manners when we were among the Dukawa at Zuru.

'We hobbled in here on Thursday,' I wrote of our arrival at Yelwa, both ponies more or less lame (the third who was still recovering from saddle sores caused by our constant wetting had been left behind at Zuru), along roads which are nothing but earth and hard pebbles. It's no country for horses. I rode up the hill to the resthouse which is about a mile and a half from the town, and as I dismounted the Union Jack was broken from the mast head, laid on by the Emir, I suppose, anyway it gave me the thrill of my life! The resthouse has a glorious view of about ten miles of the Niger and the Bussa Emurate lying over on the other bank . . . It is also worse for mosquitoes than any I've been to, they make it almost impossible to sit about after dark, and in the morning when I wake up there are four or more buzzing hungrily outside the netting – I stick the tip of my finger against it and just when they're getting their proboscis nicely engaged withdraw it again. It makes them so angry. And the place stinks with bats . . .

Colonial Postscript

Never in my life had I met so many insects. After dark one had to sit at least ten feet away from the pressure lamp to be clear of them, the lamp itself being surrounded by a circle of toads who gobbled up the casualties from the lamp as they fell to the ground. They would also accept cigarette ends, lighted or otherwise, with equal avidity. On one of these evenings I had a most unpleasant experience when a small insect flew into my inner ear and buzzed around inside there. The cook had disappeared into town and we could not find the olive oil, but managed to make up some sort of coagulant with a local wax which stilled the humming just before I lost sanity!

The Emir of Yauri was a complex character. I already knew him by reputation, as his tax was always complete within a few weeks of being announced and, in the absence of a regular mail service, he communicated with the outside world mainly by telegram; having been mildly rebuked for the length of one of these he informed the Resident in the next one that he had paid for it himself. In a letter home I reported finding him

> capable, well-educated, modern and progressive on the one hand, impatient, autocratic and conceited on the other. For ten years or more efforts have been made to provide him with a council which will do something to correct these tendencies. However, it's strange to deal with a man who really knows what's going on, signs all the vouchers, knows how much there is in any vote to last the rest of the year, knows just what is the position in respect of road construction, wears a Rolex watch and considers the motor car a greater invention than the aeroplane.

This after a two-hour conference in the resthouse which had evidently left me somewhat exhausted.

There was little to keep me in Yelwa but plenty to do outside, other than tax for a change. The M.O. who had been down on a visit from Birnin Kebbi (and had pronounced my cook's scars to be due to syphilis and nothing more serious!) had asked me

Northern Nigeria – Zuru & Yauri, 1938–9

to go up river to inspect the annual tsetse bush clearing. Tsetse fly is the carrier of sleeping sickness. 'The village I have just visited is an example of what it can do,' I wrote,

> there are only three families left of what was once a thriving settlement. Rest all dead or emigrated. I'm glad to say all these three were well. Several years ago all the places where there was thick scrub near watering places were cleared and the stumps rooted out, to a distance of about 200 yards on either side, a pretty big undertaking which was only possible by the use of forced labour, which a League of Nations convention permits for this purpose. I've now been dealing with the regrowth.

There was another inquest to be taken, this time on a mines labourer who had been killed by a fall of earth. The job took two days, on the first of which I was 'a policeman, to ask leading questions, poke my nose into things, and take evidence not on oath', and on the second

> a coroner, to write it all down, taken under oath, or oaths I should say, as there is the atheist mines manager, the Christian engineers (southerners), the various grades of Mohammedan varying from those who can repeat the Arabic words of the oath to the one who, when asked what he believed in, said "it all depends where I am", very Old Testament that, and the honest to goodness pagans whose fetish turns out to be about 70 miles away as the crow flies and under the circumstances have to be sworn as best one can.

There was no way of visiting the districts down by the big river except by boat. The Niger swarmed with canoes 'just like the Backs opposite John's,' I wrote to a Cambridge friend, himself a St John's man, 'not a white face in sight!'. My canoe was an extra large one, with an awning of sorts under which the deck chair could be placed, while the polers toiled away fore and aft, but even so it was terribly hot. It was fascinating to

Colonial Postscript

interrogate them about their fetishes, as they had none of the Hausa reserve when it came to answering questions. I sent one of the charms home to Somerset which 'cost me 2/6d in cash and quite a lot in indirect negotiations. With this you can enter the most crocodile-infested water in perfect safety – so don't be too sniffy about it!' There was no doubt about the immunity which these riverine people, unlike the townsfolk, actually enjoyed, based one can only suppose on some real understanding between the crocodiles and themselves.

All good things come to an end. 'I was just going to tell you that I would probably be in Zuru for Christmas,' I wrote,

> and here is a wire telling me that I am being relieved on the eighteenth. I suddenly feel awfully sorry that I haven't more time than that and realize that my roots, albeit rather peripatetic ones, had begun to strike in the sterile Yauri and Zuru soils. Damn!

There were all sorts of uncompleted expectations, of the new resthouse which I had designed and was building at Yelwa, the trip I had promised myself later in the month up the Ka river to try to get a glimpse of the last herd of elephant still surviving in this part of Africa. Worst of all, though not acknowledged in letters of course, was the prospect of having to mingle again with Europeans after being absent so long from their society. This, had I but known it, was a well-known symptom, and was one of the reasons why changes of posting were so often made when officers, in their own view, were becoming nicely settled.

'This is my last letter from Zuru,' I wrote a fortnight later,

> my relief is arriving in about two days and I go back to Birnin Kebbi on the lorry that will bring him here. I've just been paying off the men I'm employing on temporary building repairs, 4d a day for the labourers, 9d for the thatcher and 1/3d for the builder. Why the builder gets more than the thatcher I've never been able to fathom, it seems to me a much less skilled job. Probably when Ham got Africa – or

Northern Nigeria – Zuru & Yauri, 1938–9

was it Japhet? – he fixed their respective wages and so it has remained ever since . . . I shall look back on these past six months with very great pleasure. The tempo is much slower now than in the first few hectic weeks, tax is finished and forgotten, all the District Heads are in town and enjoying themselves, and the villagers are busy with their harvest home ceremonies, a good harvest too in spite of the locust scares earlier in the year. Some of my loads have already started off to B.K. in order to lighten the lorry and Billy (my pony) leaves early tomorrow morning.

Birnin Kebbi was something out of space and time, unashamedly feudal in every particular. The Governor was expected shortly after Christmas for the cermonial installation of the new Emir, of Gwandu as well as of Sokoto, and all thoughts of other work were laid aside while preparations were made for the great occasion.

Our strong point is the duck shooting, said to the the best in Nigeria, [His Excellency was known to be a keen shot] and there are literally thousands, we went down to look at them the other evening and it seems almost impossible they can fail us.

Nevertheless we imposed a total ban on shooting, just to be sure. My own special task was to organize a race meeting which had to be carefully rehearsed.

It may be rather a flop as far as the Governor is concerned but should be very popular with the natives – I've taught them all how to start off on the flag and didn't have to use my revolver (thank Heaven!) to recall them – I am terrified, and terrify everyone else, holding the thing in my hand even.

Finally, the invitations. 'Little did I imagine that the first invitation bearing the royal arms I received would be written in my own handwriting, but so it was, the blank cards having been

Colonial Postscript

sent out in advance for me to fill up.' The arrangements went off splendidly. H.E. got a a good bag of birds, so did the D.O. and so did I, and the last race of three furlongs was won by Billy who 'possibly had more fun than anyone, because a mare got loose from the town and he escaped from his tethering post that night, to be recovered next morning from Ambursa, about seven miles away, still in her company'.

At H.E.'s dinner party that evening the "Left Feet", as those who do not play bridge are called, played an amusing game called "Jews" demanding the minimum thought and providing the maximum excitement. It was only a little more complicated than a game popular in Sokoto in which each player is dealt a card, puts down his stake, cards are then turned up, and the highest one wins!

This was the last letter of the tour. Heavens, I remember thinking as I turned reluctantly homeward, fancy being paid to lead this marvellous life, and not having to pay to enjoy it! The great sorrow was that I was not to be reposted to Sokoto Province; but Carrow assured me that this was the hand of fate and not his own, which was some consolation. In Birnin Kebbi I managed to buy £20 of French colonial francs, a whole suitcase full, which would be useful to me on my return trip home across the Sahara, while in Sokoto my successor in the Provincial Office (where needless to say one was a Passport and Immigration Officer in addition to everything else) concocted a most impressive *laissez-passer* authorizing me to proceed almost anywhere in the world, stamping it with the most decorative seal we had available. After which I set off home – appropriately, on horseback.

Three of four days later I was waiting for the French trans-Saharan weekly bus at Niamey (an enforced stop made memorable by finding a copy of *Lady Chatterley's Lover*, in French but unexpurgated, in the resthouse). Because of the risks of breaking down or getting lost, the French confined the north-to-south traffic to two routes. One, which was the more frequented, and

Northern Nigeria – Zuru & Yauri, 1938–9

occasionally used by British officers going on or returning from leave in their own cars, went from Algiers to Zinder, north of Kano. The other, more westerly route, began at the Algerian railhead of Colomb Bechar and proceeded with five or six stops to Gao, on the Niger bend, and finished at Niamey. Both routes were closed from May to October, because of the intense heat. However, in February the air of the desert was still icy cold even at eleven o'clock in the morning, when the little bus made one of its routine halts, for the passengers to stretch their legs, and the *métis* driver to produce his radio transmission set, on which he tapped out the distance he estimated we had made since leaving the last staging post; knowing no morse, he simply tapped the numbers, one dot, three dots, four dots, 134 kilometres. One wondered whether he did it to satisfy the passengers, or there was actually someone listening at the other end. Not that it mattered on this occasion, for the journey went without a hitch.

Ten days after leaving Nigeria I was back in Somerset. I recall a dance in Bristol during this leave, at which one of the girls asked each of the men in the party, what did he do? There was an accountant, an architect, a man studying law, someone in his father's business. My turn came last. I was an Assistant District Officer in Northern Nigeria. 'Oh,' she said, pausing only for a fraction of a second, 'tea-planting, I presume.'

VI
Northern Nigeria – Lokoja, 1939–40

'There go them as 'ave made the country too 'ot for them,' observed a porter on the Liverpool wharf late in May 1939, inclining his head knowingly in the direction of an Elder Dempster mailship at the moment taking on board a respectable passenger-load of traders, missionaries and colonial civil servants for the beginning of a new tour in West Africa. That part of the world was still known to most of the older generation as the 'White Man's Grave', and it was assumed that no one would go there for choice, although it had quite ceased to deserve its reputation since the discovery of an effective vaccine against yellow fever, and was now no more unhealthy than any other part of the tropics, indeed probably rather less so in the open country to the north where most of my previous tour had been spent. This time I was bound for the less salubrious Lokoja, the administrative centre of Kabba Province, situated more or less in the middle of the country, on the banks of the Niger where it is joined by the Benue flowing in from the northeast. For a short season on the Niger and an even shorter one on the Benue, when the flood waters came rolling down and raised them by about 40 feet above the dry season level, these two rivers formed important arteries of trade, and the stern-wheel steamers of the United Africa Company made hurried journeys up-stream to bring down the stocks of palm kernel, groundnuts and products from distant inland ports in Ilorin and Adamawa. Here in the old days, on a site that was still marked by a bleak and neglected memorial, Lugard had taken over in the name of the Government from the Royal Niger Company. His

Northern Nigeria – Lokoja, 1939–40

own house had been demolished but I lived in the one next door which had been the Chief Secretary's, and was built on iron pillars and with wooden planks that had been brought out from England in sections to be assembled there. Here the original West African Frontier Force had built its barracks and trained its soldiers and buried its officers, in three extensive cemeteries which still remained, while the living had moved on elsewhere. (We were now using a fourth, where I buried at dawn one day one of the old coasters who had been too long in the country to bother about inoculations.) Lokoja, once an important centre, had been bypassed by new routes which no longer followed the unhealthy river valleys. But it was still a place of some consequence, being one of the five 'townships' in Northern Nigeria, that is to say an area excluded from the jurisdiction of any chief or chief-in-council, and administered directly under the Government by a local authority. This was to be me, for the next nine months, and once more I was given the powers of a magistrate to be able to exercise it. As usual, it involved a number of incidental activites – like giving Christian burial to the bodies on which, the day before, one had held a coroner's inquest.

'I have thoroughly enjoyed this voyage,' I wrote to my mother in the first letter home from the new station, 'though the last two days of the trip are always something of an anticlimax, as so many of the passengers get off on the Gold Coast.' No doubt I had in mind one in particular of the passengers who disembarked there, having come out on a holiday to stay with the wife of the Manager of the Ashanti Gold Mines, though it was not till six months later that I mentioned her name or even her existence! From now on the main news went to Patricia Booth, and my mother only got what was left, though I don't think it was this fact, but rather the nature of the job itself, which caused my letters home during this subsequent period to be relatively dull and uninspired. First impressions were obviously not at all favourable.

I had to leave the train at about 6.30 a.m. to get into a lorry which spent most of the day getting here, the distance being about 230 miles. It is awful to speak Hausa and be met by an absolutely blank look on the native face; my driver and his two assistants, all of whom wore preparatory school caps of blue and yellow alternate stripes ... talked a little English and a lot of something I am credibly informed was Yoruba.

The work was essentially not too different from that of the Provincial Office in Sokoto, though it was more independent since it did not come directly under the Resident. Once again one was confronted with a whole mass of Treasury work which it was impossible to supervise directly, and there was the same ultimate responsibility for any counterfeit coinage. This we dealt with in summary fashion by breaking it up on sight – much to the chagrin of those presenting it – or sometimes nailing it to the counter as a warning to those who called at the office. Later I had some of the collection converted into a tray by a local brass smith, who pricked his name 'Amadu Bida' and the words *Aikina Makeri* 'the Smith, I made it' on the back. I presented it in 1974 to the Commonwealth Institute in London. As for the accountancy work I was lucky enough early on to detect one of the clerks in an act of fraud and had him successfully prosecuted, thus creating a reputation for Argus-eyed vigilance which was really quite undeserved. It is sometimes good advice, and not only in Nigeria, to make a nuisance of oneself to start with in order to save a lot of trouble later.

The main difference between Lokoja and Sokoto was in the court work and as I was reading for the Bar at the time (but never completed the course because of the war) this was of particular interest to me. The township was only a small area but the people were quarrelsome and litigious, so there was quite a lot for the magistrate to do, under both the civil and criminal law. Records of cases heard had to be transcribed and sent to Northern Provinces headquarters where they were automatically reviewed and quite often quashed on technical grounds – a humiliating experience for the magistrate concerned, only to be avoided by the exercise of great care, allied with a certain amount of ingenuity. Thus it might be advisable to allude in the summing up to the demeanour of the defendant, when the case

Northern Nigeria – Lokoja, 1939–40

against him seemed on paper a little incomplete, as this was one of the facts that Kaduna couldn't possibly check. A fascinating aspect of the court work consisted of the committal proceedings for offences which carried too heavy a sentence for the magistrate and had to be reserved until the assizes; there was much to be learnt at the trial about what should or should not have been done at the preliminary hearing.

Outside the township area lay the native town of Lokoja – the original for Dickens' 'Borrio-Boola-Gha' in *Bleak House* – forming part of the Kabba Division but looked after by the Local Authority on behalf of the District Officer, who was stationed elsewhere in the Province. The Town Council met once a fortnight, on Saturday afternoons, when I would skip tennis at the club and bicycle down to attend their meetings, but it was difficult to make much headway, for the town councillors were a cantankerous lot, by and large, and did not respond to the mild joke or witticism which so often saved the situation when one was dealing with Hausas. The town's modest budget allowed only one new capital project and in 1939, it had been decided, we were to move with the times and have our first public latrine, that world-wide monument to enlightenment and progress. The only problem was, where to put it? The town, squeezed between the river and the steep hill at the back, was overcrowded already, and public latrines in the tropics are not nice neighbours. So it appeared, to me at any rate, that the only place where it could be put was on the foreshore, where it would stand well away from the rest of the buildings but, as a compensating disadvantage, it would also be submerged or at least rendered inaccessible by the rising waters of the Niger at the peak of its flood for two or three weeks every year. Which is what happened, and it was bad luck that this time coincided with the visit of the Chief Commissioner, to whom I did not dare point out 'Morley's folly', standing isolated, and looking decidedly incongruous, several yards out from the river bank.

War broke out in Europe some three months after the beginning of this tour, but did not at first have much effect on us except that the arrival of letters was much delayed. As there

Colonial Postscript

were no local Nigerian newspapers, and radio reception was often so bad as to be almost impossible, this made us feel very cut off in Lokoja from the rest of the world, though not so bad as it was to be later out on my own in the bush, where night after night I sat out under the full moon wondering whether its light was guiding enemy bombers to their targets across the English Channel. The Nigerian government brought out a mass of emergency regulations, local income tax went up from 1 per cent to 1½ per cent, and was expected to climb to 2½ per cent (sixpence in the £!), while

> every European in the country has had a copy of a message from the Governor exhorting him to do all sorts of things, economize etc., and more particularly in view of longer tours, harder work (this hasn't come my way yet) and the importance of keeping fit, cutting out that immemorial custom in Nigeria of serving food an hour or more after guests have arrived, which usually leads to "the consumption of more alcohol than is desirable or, in most cases, desired . . ." – the Governor always writes as he speaks, in a very fluent manner. It is much laughed at, as one might expect, but given a lead from that quarter people are quite likely to pay attention to it, and it will be a very good thing if they do.

About this time I had a letter from Freya Stark, the authoress, explorer and friend of A.B. whom I had first met at the Besse's house in the south of France and once or twice since; she wrote from Aden that she was attached to the Ministry of Information and travelling round the tribes. I think there was some suggestion that I might join her there. However, it was impossible at that time even to think of getting a release and although I had gone through the motions of applying for it I had not tried very hard, reckoning on somehow getting home on leave and then being able to join the Royal Air Force in England (I had been trained to be a pilot by the Cambridge University Air Squadron). 'I'd be glad of a change from Lokoja but know definitely that I shall be in here for Christmas,' I wrote towards the end of the year.

1 A Zabirma from Dosso (Niger)

2 Moman Kalgo from Sokoto (Nigeria)

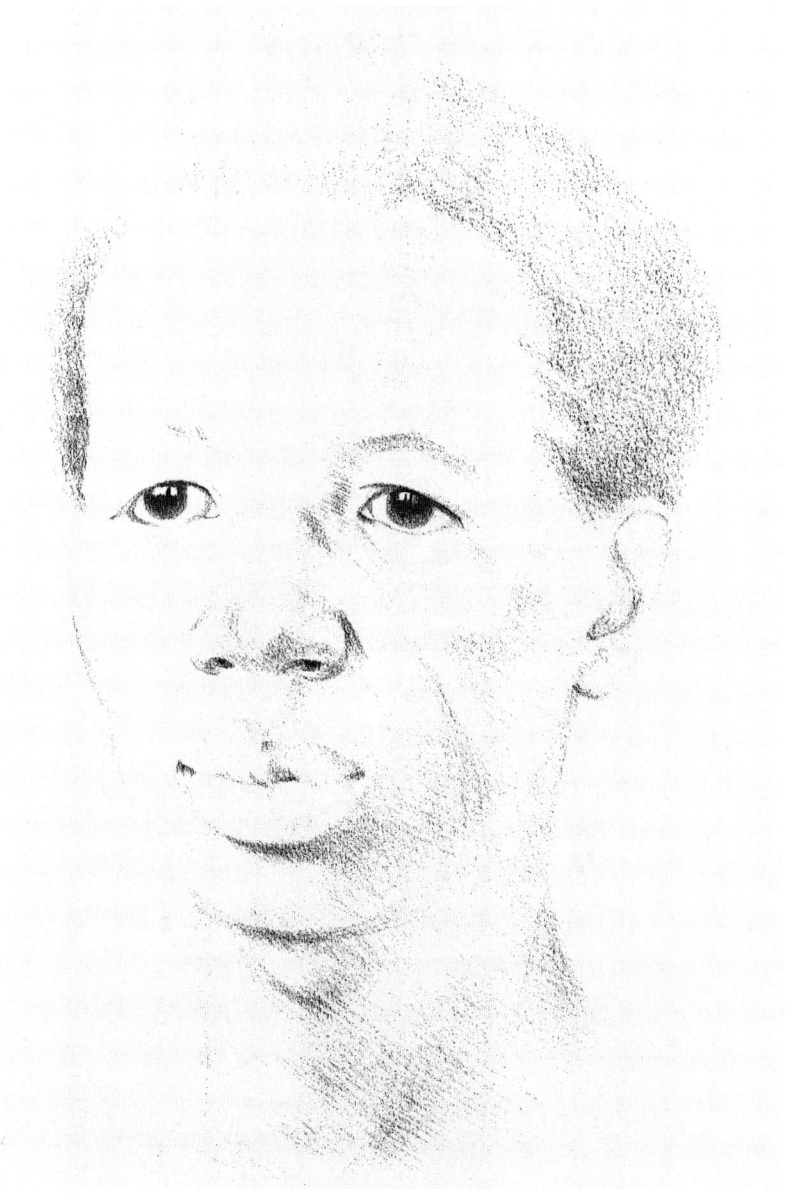

3 Awuni Frafra from Mamprusi (Gold Coast/Ghana)

4 Tahiru Wenchi from Brong Ahafo (Gold Coast/Ghana)

5 Ahmadu Buzu from Gao (Fr. Sudan/Mali)

6 Kofi Misah II Pankesihene (Gold Coast/Ghana)

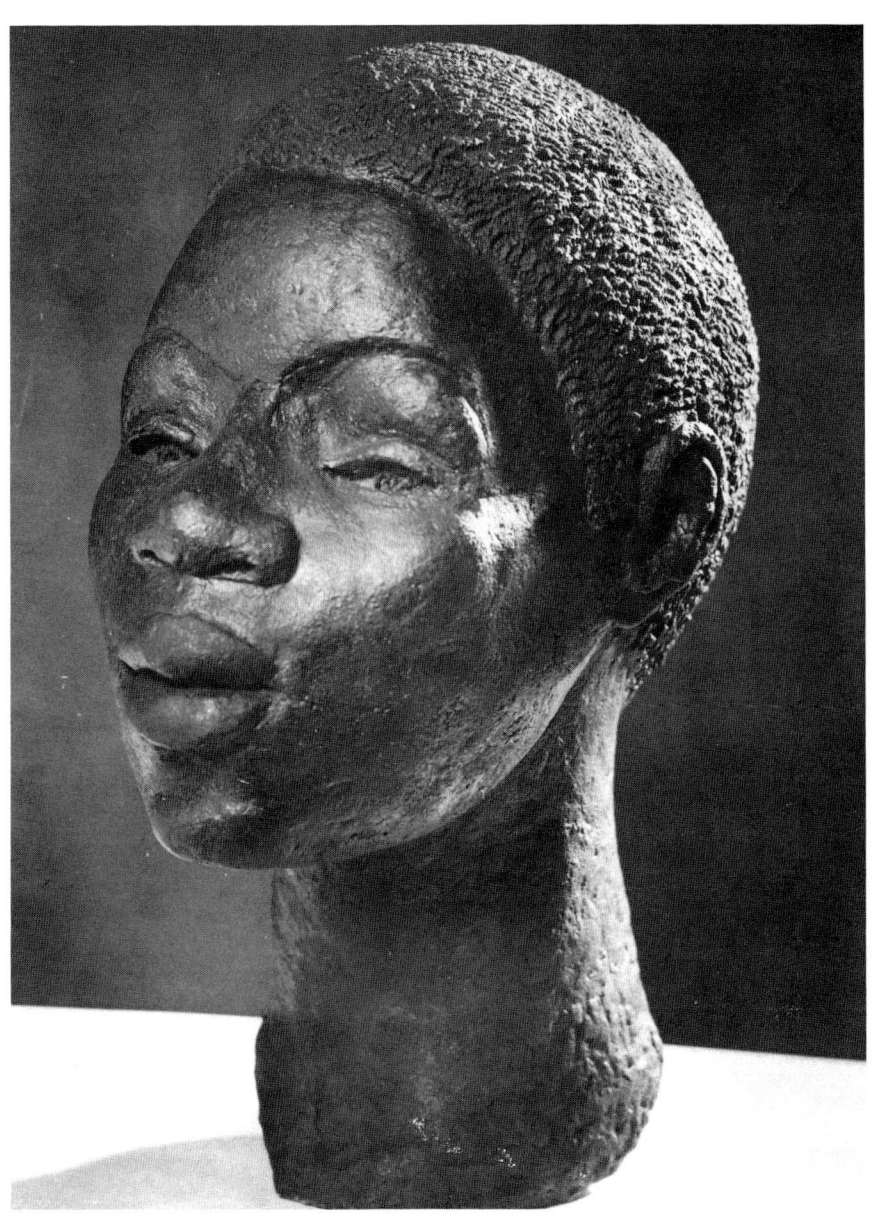
7 Salonika (Fr. Togoland/Togo)

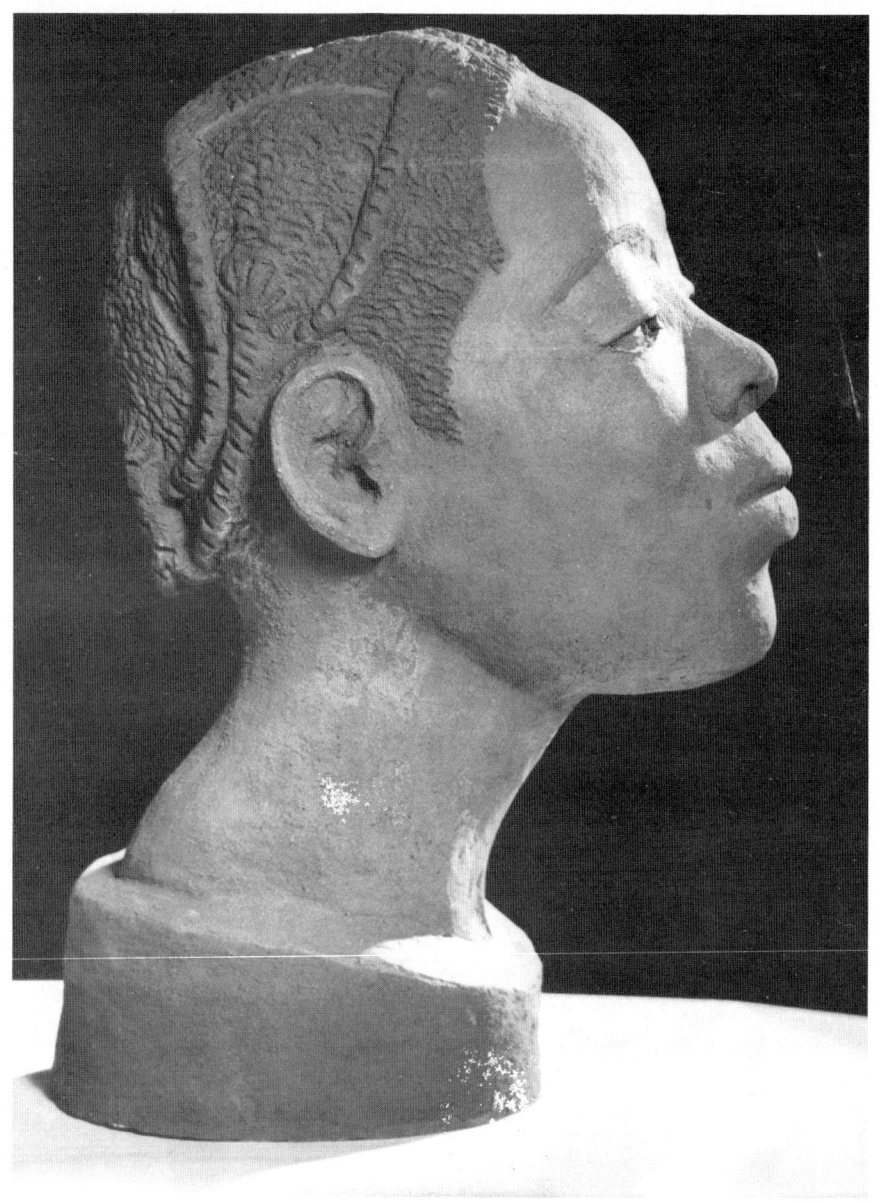

8 Beatrice the carpenter's daughter from Accra (Gold Coast/Ghana)

Northern Nigeria – Lokoja, 1939–40

Probably when I do get any touring I shall have a stomachfull; Reynolds who passed through here on the way home early this week had spent virtually twelve months in isolation and one didn't have to speak to him twice to realize that that was a great deal too long. Solitude in these areas must be very much more real than it is in the north where the black man has not infrequently the degree of civilization – whatever I mean by that – to elevate him to a companion.

Reynolds had been in Ankpa district over on the other side of the river, and in April 1940 I learnt that I was to follow him there.

Ankpa is another "deserted village', *à la* Zuru, once full of soldiery but now a scene of departed glory. It has a rainfall of 76 inches and the reputation of being the most backward area in the Northern Provinces. Even seven maids with seven mops would find it beyond them; one A.D.O. congratulates himself if he can keep it from getting any worse or, if he doesn't succeed in doing that, reflects that there's not much worse it can get. So says local gossip. The area is also covered by a peculiar set of missionaries whose quarrels among themselves government has tried in vain to compose, and give a most unChristian example of brotherhood to the local natives (who, as you will have gathered, have not a little to learn in this respect). There are also some German R.C. missionaries who are not interned but probably find their activities considerably restricted owing to complete absence of funds. And my old friend, Sgt Isa Sokoto, commands a detachment of police, so I shall have someone to talk Hausa to.

Sgt. Isa had been the prosecutor in the magistrate's court at Lokoja, and he gave me a warm welcome when I arrived in Ankpa, where together we managed to get ourselves out of an awkward situation, as will be recounted in the next chapter.

VII
Northern Nigeria – Ankpa, 1940–1

Relief at escaping from the humdrum activity of the Local Authority's office and delight at being on tour again, even if it was only in the Ankpa Division, are apparent in the next batch of letters. They cover a period of about five or six months and again will be taken out of order to make the story more intelligible. Conditions here were different in many respects from those in Sokoto, as I soon discovered.

> Travelling with a tent is not nearly so convenient as stopping in native huts and resthouses (the latter are rare in this Division and the former, like their owners, are so filthy that I have no wish to use them). You can't let the carriers go ahead with the tent until you are out of it yourself, and as their rate of travelling is not over three miles an hour you are likely to get there before them and have to sit about until they arrive. However they are now so well trained that all the loads are bound up before I'm "called", and the moment I emerge from the tent all hands are laid on the pegs and guy ropes so that they have it packed up and away before I've finished shaving. It's also very different to Hausa country where you arrive at a place to find wood and water, eggs and a chicken ready for slaughter. Here it is only after I have arrived and made a "scene" that these things are forthcoming. Same in everything, orders never carried out unless one goes oneself to supervise, and even then badly.

There were no horses in these latitudes, though this turned out to be less of a deprivation than expected. 'Bicycling along bush

Northern Nigeria – Ankpa, 1940–1

paths I find a much more enjoyable form of travelling than I imagined,' I wrote to my sister.

It's like driving a small car fast along a country lane, you are not going very fast really but by the time you've done ten miles flat out along one of the blind bush paths you feel you've had all the thrills you want for one morning. A complication one doesn't have in car driving is that the well-mannered A.D.O. feels it incumbent on him to say *Awa*, the local word of greeting, to everyone he meets on the road and the combination of speed and politeness was too much for me the other day; I raised my eye from the track to say *Awa* to one of the local beauties and ran hard into a hidden snag with my left pedal. I landed flat at her feet. Was she surprised! I have a special "bicycle boy" who, except on main roads where I too easily outdistance him, takes it from me when I dismount and pushes it up hills, through sand, or lifts and carries it where the ground is very rough indeed. Wear and tear is pretty hard; in two months I've got through two tyres, one pedal, two hubs with innumerable ball bearings, and one saddle. The last was when my boy leant the bicycle against the mud wall of a rest house and we found the next day that the white ants had almost eaten it to bits. They have unexpected tastes.

My first letter from Ankpa is dated 6 May 1940. 'Last time I wrote was from Idah,' it begins. (Idah on the Niger was the divisional headquarters and Ankpa lay some way beyond it to the northeast.)

I only stayed there two or three days, to hear some P.I.s (preliminary investigations) for the D.O. One was on the well-mixed charges of practising witchcraft for reward, pawning (accepting a person as security for debt – a form of slave dealing quite common in these parts) and attempted bribery of a police constable! He was committed to the High Court for all three. The other was a not very clear manslaughter case which I didn't finish ... Here in Ankpa I have a small contingent of Government police to guard me against the wild Igalas and investigate the fairly frequent murders. This *is* a place! I was shaken for a moment when all twelve of the prisoners in the small prison here rose like one man when asked if any of them wanted their cases reviewed, but it would have surprised me less if I had then, as I have now, spent two full days doing absolutely no other work but listen to complainants and risen in the afternoon to find those still present about double those who had been there in the morning. "And you wait until it is generally known that there is a touring officer here," said my messenger darkly. Practically every case where the parties can afford it goes to appeal, and those who can't go to the A.D.O. instead. The courts are so dilatory and I fear corrupt that even if a correct decision is given by accident it is questioned immediately. Unfortunately I had no one to hand over to me, but gather that by the time the mob has grown really large the moment has come to go out and tour the districts, to the annoyance of the complainants who haven't the energy to follow one there, and the joy of others who have been too lazy to come into Ankpa.

Comparing this state of affairs with the true north I put the difference down to religion. 'Islam has much intrinsic merit and is fairly well organized,' I wrote to my mother, choosing my words with care for someone who looked on Mohammedans as heretics, persons to be prayed for perhaps but hardly to be respected,

> it had the chance of sustaining the impact of modern ideas better than the local pagan culture which as far as I know at present was an elaborate priest-king hierarchy bound up with much heathen ritual. I don't know what the central idea was, but presumably it was weak enough for the first bright young sparks to say "We don't believe" and get away with it. (The Zuru one was much stronger and is fighting its inevitably losing battle with great tenacity.) So religious sanctions went,

Northern Nigeria – Ankpa, 1940–1

and with them the respect for traditional authority which went with them – and that's the discipline of any community but especially one as conservative as the African. Time alone will show whether the new authority with which we are clothing the somewhat reluctant "Onus" is keeping pace with the prestige they are losing elsewhere, and the missions which have only local influence at present are of course as always working on democratic lines and hasten the process of disintegration ... Tomorrow or the next day I'm going to Ofante, a village situated in a wedge of territory running into the Southern Provinces which has acquired a bad reputation for child stealing, highway robbery, occasional murders and general disobedience to government. Some 15 years ago there was quite a serious affair there, but in those days one could do more and fewer questions were asked; now we have to rely more on bluff. The Ata of Igala who is our local potentate went there and made the fatal mistake of bribing them so as to allow themselves to be counted at all, news of which has of course spread all round the division. The people are poor but pay hardly any tax, they tap the palm trees for the palm wine (which kills the trees) instead of collecting and selling the kernels. I sent a message there this morning to announce that the tax collecting season would begin there on Friday next, so we shall see! Further instalments of this thrilling serial in our next issue.

A week passed, and I wrote again.

I had the great satisfaction two days ago of seeing a plan which depended on the two elements of bluff and surprise succeed beyond my utmost expectations. In the middle of dense bush where they could have lain hidden for months if they had had the least suspicion of what was about to happen we lifted our five wanted men, these were the people who had been identified as leading the resistance to the payment of tax, from a crowd of three or four hundred strong, taken completely by surprise, and got them away in safety. I can't tell you how relieved I am as the whole area has had its eyes on this one village, and the outcome has diminished the trouble which might have arisen elsewhere. My old friend Sergeant Isa is very good value in a show of this kind, and was confident as though his four men had been a regiment, which was very comforting when we were all waiting for zero hour. It was one of the most unpleasant places I've ever had to stay. My tent was pitched in the middle of a compound surrounded by high plantain trees which didn't let in a breath of air. Outside every hut (from which the unfortunate inhabitants had of course been evicted) were signs of "fetish" worship, sometimes a little thatched dolls' house with a broken earthenware pot or two containing dried yam, sometimes a bottle stuck upright in a wall of dried clay. In the middle of the compound is a hollowed-out depression into which the rainwater collects. This is the water supply. As it doesn't rain during the winter, water is stored in pots from one wet season to another, and becomes indescribably disgusting – the colour of tomato soup and the smell of a sewer. It didn't surprise me to find more horrible sores and illnesses than I've ever seen anywhere else in Nigeria.

As to how the surprise was achieved I may have thought it better not to say too much in a letter. Briefly what happened was this. Tax was announced at a first meeting at which the villagers were truculent, as expected, but the A.D.O. must have seemed to them mild and conciliatory. Another meeting was called the next day and, in the meanwhile, each of my five police identified for himself one of the five ringleaders for whom he was to be responsible. The meeting on the following day was a tougher affair, with the villagers now emboldened to advance frivolous reasons for not paying tax at all, to which the A.D.O. replied that a warning had been given and, since it had not been heeded, the discussion must be concluded. Saying this he rose in his chair to dismiss the meeting and, as he did so, the five police walked into the crowd and each arrested his man. The crowd fled, taken completely by surprise, the police fixed bayonets

Northern Nigeria – Ankpa, 1940–1

(their rifles contained no ammunition!) and escorted the captives safely away, although a half-hearted attempt was made to ambush them. Back in Ankpa we stuck the five men in gaol and waited for trouble, which was not long in coming – with petitioners coming first to Ankpa, where needless to say they met with a stony reception, and then to the District Officer and Resident, who undertook to investigate and in due course did so. But these things take time, and while the wheels of justice were being set in motion and awkward questions began to be asked as to the grounds on which the five men of Ofante were being detained in custody, the villagers' nerve had broken, tax came rolling in, faster indeed than we were able to issue receipts for it, and it was possible to reply that they had already been released. They bore no ill-will, nor the rest of the village either, and on later occasions when I revisited it no police escort went with me.

Even after this successful foray I was still much preoccupied with tax for the next month or so. Because of shipping difficulties the staffing position was still fairly good, but with a war on it was likely to be upset at any moment and the one thing not to be left undone was tax collection, in case the division might be left at short notice without its political incumbent. 'I am now touring the fourth of my seven districts,' I wrote just before my twenty-sixth birthday,

> the remaining three will have to be visited next month. The people have the money alright but in many cases have come to regard it as their privilege not to pay anything until the touring officer has visited them and taken some fairly drastic action to make them. Only two of the four District Heads I have seen can be safely left to do the work themselves. The others are too irresponsible to be very much good; a village says, "yes, we'll pay, but we must have a feast first", which means that every adult male gets blind drunk for a day or so and spends a good deal of his money on the beer or palmwine consumed. Another village has been allowed to go off on a hunting expedition which may last two or three weeks. The

Colonial Postscript

District Head appears repentant enough when taken to task for his slackness in allowing such things to happen, and the next you hear of him is that he is half-seas-over himself.

All this was going on against the background of the dramatic unfolding of the war in Europe, about which I heard snippets of information scribbled down by the Acting D.O. in Idah as he heard them over the radio and sent to me by the weekly messenger, and read about in detail in the airmail *Times* when this reached me seven weeks later. The paper arrived irregularly in weekly and fortnightly batches and, as it was all I had to read, and a great solace in my somewhat lonely existence, it was carefully rationed, one paper per day. My parents had arranged for it to be sent to me which may be one of the reasons why it was often mentioned when I was short of other news. Thus I was amused by the history student whose letter in the paper

proves to his own satisfaction that the Norwegians succeed in repelling an invader every 300 years and cites examples in the 11th, 14th and 17th centuries, and suggests that it's just going to happen again – this coincides with radio news of the final withdrawal from Narvik. I have been enjoying immensely the letters from big-game hunters, some obviously not so skilled with the pen, who have been rallying round in the correspondence on how to deal with parachutists. A Mr Naish writes "the Winchester is used by professional kangaroo hunters and is very effective at moderate range". Another one wants "12 bore guns loaded with buck-shot" and an even more ingenious lady suggests that postmen should all be provided with firearms and trained how to use them, "here is a standing army already organised". All very serious no doubt but I'm afraid I couldn't help laughing. The local Igala is considerably alarmed at the prospect of parachutists and will hardly be comforted by my assuring him that he is not of the least importance to anyone; the word "parachute" being translated into the vernacular by the word meaning "umbrella" this has added one more peculiar conception to their already singular notions about the nature

Northern Nigeria – Ankpa, 1940–1

of modern warfare. The reaction to a crisis here would be for everyone to run to bush until it was all over and as even on the one occasion when I used a little force it took them three or four days to drift back; if a parachutist were once reported they wouldn't be seen or heard of for weeks.

In order to curb these rumours we tried the experiment of a public reading of the Hausa newspaper – which a fair number of the population could understand, even though they did not speak the language – by the senior court scribe. This was a great success, and did much to still their fears. These people of the southern forests had, as I have already explained, quite a different mentality from the Hausas, who were persons of discipline, tradition and order. On one of my visits to Idah I was able to catch up with the northern news from a friend who had just returned from there and

> had much news of many friends, European and African. The Waziri (Vizir) of Sokoto, who is a dyed-in-the-wool old aristocrat, if ever there was one, summed up the European situation rather aptly by snorting that that was what came of choosing one's leaders out of the *talakawa* (nobodies) like the *mashafin penti* (house decorator, i.e. Hitler) instead of from one of the proved old families. No danger of that sort of thing happening in Sokoto Emirate, begad!

He also brought me news from Mallam Bello, the indefatigable messenger from Birnin Kebbi who had accompanied me everywhere on my Zuru touring, and had written to ask me for a pair of spectacles. The local United Africa Company store in Idah stocked three varieties of these; weak, medium and strong. I had taken a chance and sent him the strong ones, with which he was highly delighted.

One of the commonplaces about the British colonial system is that political officers soon became fiercely proprietorial about the people among whom they worked. Primitive they might be in habits and behaviour, but interest deepened the longer one spent with them. Unfortunately nearly all one's knowledge had to be acquired from scratch; of all the countless touring officers who had preceded me in Ankpa none had left any record of his experiences or, if he had, it had been removed to the district office at Idah, where it was as surely lost as if it had never existed. One of them had been an amateur surveyor of some skill, whose map of the villages and paths in the district was one of my most valued possessions. Villages they purported to be, but when one arrived at the intersection of paths where they were supposed to be situated there was no sign of them. Another odd feature was the frequency with which names were repeated. After a little while the truth dawned on me; they were not place names at all, but names of days of the week from which one could tell when a market was due to be held on this spot. (I wondered whether the map-maker had been aware of this.) This was a big help in working out one's touring programme in order to meet the people – always providing one remembered that the Igala week consisted of four days only, so that a market held on Monday and Friday this week would be held on Tuesday and Saturday next week, and so on. It was quite confusing.

'There are markets big and small within range of every village,' I wrote, so that the villagers could if they wanted to go to a different one every day. They play a most important part in the economic and social life of the people, for besides being the only place where buying and selling is done it is also the pub, the press and radio, the fashion centre, the post office and the first meeting place of the amorous youth and maiden. While I was going round this one and visiting the stalls of the sellers of imported cloth I came across one with the makers' label still attached "Made in Manchester, Igala pattern"! I should never have credited an English manufacturer with being so enterprising.

'I was prepared for an idle and probably rather boring Sunday as tax is finished in this village,' I wrote from another district a fortnight later,

Northern Nigeria – Ankpa, 1940–1

but it has brought quite a lot of interest and having nothing else to write about I'll fall back on the usual "last resource" and describe routine work which was – as it nearly always is in Igala – listening to complaints. They started off this morning with what promised to be quite a gruesome murder – body on the road, blood on the head etc. – but turned out after examining three of four witnesses to be much more likely accidental death. The corpse had been suffering from a complaint, which I identified at a hazard as gallstones, which general opinion seemed to think was quite likely to cause a man to die suddenly, and had fallen down on rocky ground where he had bruised his head, had been discovered and decently buried by the neighbouring villagers, including some relatives, none of whom suspected foul play; then two months later an old stiff comes along and says "dirty work at the crossroads" or the equivalent in Igala and two or three hours have to be spent in patiently extracting statements from the various people who were present and have just about as much idea of how to tell a continuous and coherent story as fly!

Then there were two women, both of whom thought they had been sold into slavery. The ordinary form of matrimonial arrangement is such an entirely mercenary affair that the dividing line is often rather difficult to see and in the case of one of them it soon became clear that the marriage had been perfectly in accord with native custom and that what she was really seeking was a ruling from me which might taint her second marriage (the alleged slavery) with illegality and make the relatives of the second husband, with whom she had lived happily until his death, chary of enforcing their claims to her as a wife by inheritance. Personally I thought that she rather overrated her charms and that her relations in law would no longer consider her a marketable asset, so it was decided we would wait and see what happened. The other woman told a much more convincing story but there were one or two unlikely features about it and it will have to be seen what the accused has to say. Child stealing, and child selling is not at all uncommon on the southern boundary between the Igalas

Colonial Postscript

and Ibos. The Igala would not hesitate to sell his wife or child if it looked like being a profitable transaction. I wouldn't put it past him to sell his parents if the opportunity occurred! You can easily imagine how much more difficult such crimes are to suppress when the social conscience is not really against them.

After that there was a deputation from the inhabitants of Agariga, a nearby village. Their wives said they wanted to perform a new fetish which involved the sacrifice of a horse and a cow. The Onu (District Head) had not given his decision but appeared to be against it, chiefly I think on the grounds that horses have only been used in ceremonies connected with the death of important people and he didn't want it vulgarized. They could kill as many cows as they liked. It was a very extraordinary request because even in the burial ceremonies the horse had never been killed, this new idea is obviously one that has been borrowed from the Ibos in the south, who unfortunately sacrifice a good many every year. So I got the Ata's representative, who is senior in rank to the Onu, to confirm the Onu's refusal and tell them to continue in their customs and not go borrowing other people's. This he did, rather to their disgust, for it was clear that the mention of their wives was only a blind, they had thought it out for themselves. Anyway I can go to bed tonight satisfied that I've earned one good mark from the R.S.P.C.A. – a big one too, because the Ibo method of killing horses is a particularly brutal one – even though the point of view of cruelty to animals was much too advanced an idea to be worth referring to! The whole question of fetishes, feasts to one's ancestors, worship of the "God" present in stones and certain big trees, and the efficacy of charms is one that you soon find yourself discussing with complete seriousness and absence of mental reserve, in the presence of people who really believe in these things and consider them of immense importance. I've been investigating the forms of oath taking in the different courts and observing with interest the variations in them; what involves careful purification in one place is a matter of no

Northern Nigeria – Ankpa, 1940–1

importance in another. I can fully understand the appeal of anthropological field work among intact tribal societies, which I never could before, though I still think it's difficult if not impossible to combine with the work of an administrative officer.

The next letter was written from Ofanti,

one of the first villages I visited after arriving in this area about three months ago. Tax being finished we deposed the Onu, a thing I've been wanting to do ever since I first came here and saw him, which means a job of work if not for myself for my successor since that Igalas should agree on the choice of a candidate when more than one presents himself is the sort of miracle that never happens. The Resident Councillor who travels round with me is quite pleased with the course of events since there are many bribes to be looked for. He's a nice old fellow but unfortunately can't be trusted even as far as you can see him.

In the same letter I mentioned that I had got my supplies of stores at last but only after running out of marmalade, coffee, flour, milk and tobacco which had caused breakfast to be a rather uninteresting meal. Nigeria was beginning to feel the pinch from delayed or lost cargoes and the Lagos stores 'don't feel themselves obliged to make any special effort for the up-country customer they never see'. The following week notepaper had run out as well, and the next few letters are on foolscap leaves torn out of exercise books. The effects of the war were beginning to touch even the Igala backwoods.

I've now got a new odd job added to the miscellaneous list, that of paying the monthly allotments to dependants of soldiers on active service. Nearly every soldier in the W.A.F.F. when it was here must have made the most of his opportunities, and as a result on the first day of the month the office was a seething mass of women, every one of whom seemed to be called Hadeja, which didn't make it any easier (especially as roughly every fifth soldier calls himself Isa Zuru, Moman Kano or Garba Zaria). When I'd got them all sorted out I besought them whatever they did not to call their daughters Hadeja, and even they saw the joke!

At this time many new battalions of the Nigeria Regiment were being formed, and all District Officers were urged to help with recruiting. The Army laid down three conditions; the man must be in good health, he should be able to pass an intelligence test and he must know the points of the compass. My poor Igalas would have to be excluded therefore; they had no idea about north, south, east and west. So we carried out our recruiting first thing in the morning. 'Ask him where the east is,' I said to the messenger in Hausa. 'Tell the white man where the sun rises,' translated the messenger into Igala. The would-be soldier pointed to the sun at that moment coming up in the east, wondering whether all white men asked such silly questions. 'And the west?' That was easy too, and though he failed on north and south he had got half-marks. All the Igalas were excellent on intelligence tests; if I turned them round and asked them to describe the objects on the other side of the room or the people standing in the office compound they were able to do so minutely and with the greatest accuracy. As for health, all I could do was to ask each candidate if he had ever fallen out of a palm tree, this being a common accident suffered by young men when they went up them to tap the palm wine. If he had, the note to the doctor warned him to look out for any internal injuries.

Five months earlier when I arrived in Ankpa I had found the garden round the tumbledown old bungalow in a state of complete neglect, but with the help of prison labour, seeds sent out from home and my own efforts the place had been quite transformed. 'It is looking *lovely*,' I wrote,

> I can honestly say that I've never seen one in the country so full of flowers ... balsam about 18 inches high and each of

Northern Nigeria – Ankpa, 1940–1

them with three or four branches simply covered with blossom. You can see them a mile away. Zinnias three or four inches across, marigolds and petunias; they're the only ones out yet but there are others coming on. And out of the vegetable garden I had all in one day radishes, lettuce, cucumber, carrots, beans and new potatoes . . . Consequently if my time is up here I should not be in the least surprised!

Tax being finished in the Ankpa district I fully expected to be transferred somewhere else. One mission which had been mentioned was a big 'tax palaver' at a place called Adoru 'where a deputation of some 500 women were promised a reinvestigation and possibly a reassessment. A less enjoyable job can hardly be imagined as they are a truculent lot and very much a frontier problem. It could be an extremely interesting one though'. The District Officer at Idah was in need of help and I had already been there for a week to undertake the prosecution in a murder case in which it was particularly important to make a good impression on the judge, who was to be one of the two examiners for the Intermediate Standard in Hausa which I was to take when the case was over. 'The court sessions went off very well,' I wrote later,

> the skull of the murdered man was produced and identified and even if the accused had made any attempt to deny it there would have been abundant evidence to go on (a plea of "not guilty" is always entered as a matter of course in a murder trial). The judge did not wear robes, nor put on his black cap, the court was practically empty, the conclusion foreseen and the slow, clear voice of the judge speaking in Hausa as undramatic as anything you could imagine, but still it is an awful moment when the play of words and arguments is over and you all stand up while the sentence of death is passed. I felt very green for a moment, and was glad there was no occasion to say anything.
>
> I had my intermediate Hausa exam the next day and they considered me just good enough to let me through on token

marks of 61 per cent – 60 per cent being a pass. (This was an exam one was not expected to take until one had spent many years in the country, the lenience of the examiners would no doubt have been due to the fact that there was a war on.) They managed to raise some quite respectable mallams with whom I discoursed, interpreted, explained and interrogated for close on two hours. Leonard (the D.O.) produced the following gem from the building regulations made under the Township Ordinance for translation at sight: "not more than one third of the area of a compound shall be covered by buildings intended for human habitation, the distance between houses shall be not less than twelve feet, the internal diameter less than fourteen feet, or the floor area less than 120 square feet etc.'. Try to interpret this in a language possessing only one vague linear measurement corresponding to a cubit, and no measurement of area at all and you find that you have to paraphrase very freely!

Leonard, my D.O., who had at one time been in the army seemed to have some intimation that my call-up could be expected fairly soon and it was no surprise when the bicycle messenger brought in a note from him one day shortly after my return to Ankpa – scribbled on the back of an old Provincial Court form, since we had had no new stocks of paper for months – telling me to report to the military depot at Enugu in a few days time. 'I expect you are pleased?,' he added in a footnote and, lacking as always imagination or even curiosity about the future, I expect I was. In my case the Army were apparently prepared to waive knowledge of the points of the compass and the intelligence test, but they still insisted on a medical inspection, so I had to go and see the African doctor in Idah. He passed me as fit, without ever enquiring if I had fallen out of a palm tree!

VIII
Northern Nigeria – Kano – RWAFF, 1940–1

The British regular officers seconded to the Royal West African Frontier Force before the war had been attracted by the low cost of living, with opportunities for shooting and polo, rather than by any prospect of seeing active service. In 1940, after the military defeat of France, when all the French colonies surrounding Nigeria except Chad in the northeast fell under the control of the Vichy government, the frontier once more became a reality. Even then however it appeared that if Nigerians had to fight they were more likely to do so overseas than in defence of their own territory – in Abyssinia or some part of the Middle East we thought, wrongly as it turned out, for it was to Burma that they were eventually sent, though there was no word of this possibility at the time of which I am writing. In 1940 the regiment was being expanded very fast with all the difficulties and problems that arise on these occasions, and are particularly acute in an African context. Featherstone, the Resident of Kabba Province, had a delightful story about an incident which occurred while he was travelling to Kaduna on the railway and sharing a compartment with a senior military officer. At one of the many stops en route a subaltern, who was in a compartment further down the train, came forward to report.

'Just worked out that calculation, Sir,' he said, 'we shall need 3.73 lorries to move all those stores from A to B.'

'Very good,' said the senior officer, 'that's better than I expected.'

At the next station the subaltern was back again. 'Revised

calculation, Sir,' he said. 'Should be 37.3 lorries. Slipped a decimal point.' One got the impression that not all the errors were corrected quite so speedily!

After living so long in isolation and independence it took some adjustment to get used to the crowded conditions where four or five and sometimes as many as nine Europeans were all sharing the same quarters, although

> we manage to "muck in" rather more successfully than our servants do, who have only five rooms between the nine of them, and sorting out between them is a delicate matter, since on the one hand north and south don't get on at all well, and on the other you feel that greybeards ought to have rooms to themselves if possible.

To begin with it was even 'a grand change to be in a place where there are many other people from all parts of the country, a good number of whom I haven't seen since the voyage out in 1937'.

> The army hasn't stood still since O.T.C. days and it's harder to forget old drill movements than it would be to start at the beginning and learn new ones. The parade ground stuff isn't given much time on this course though there must be something inside one which likes the idea of smartness, otherwise we shouldn't be at pains to drill twice as briskly when one of the other squads is in sight or hearing. Everywhere we are reminded of that automaton referred to in the drill books as "the trained man", a sort of warrior's Colonel Bogey who can fire more rounds per minute, throw more grenades and "appreciate" more "situations" in a quicker time than seems either right or decent.

This was a short training course, and it was taken for granted that most if not all those taking part would be commissioned. We rubbed up our arms drill, were introduced to the Bren gun, learnt some elementary tactics and prepared defensive positions.

Northern Nigeria – Kano – RWAFF, 1940–1

This remains in my mind as a unique occasion, since up to that time one could have travelled the length and breadth of Africa without ever seeing Europeans perform a manual task, and here were some two dozen of us set to dig holes for ourselves in the tough laterite soil with pick and shovel. The servants each one of us had brought with him hovered solicitously watching their masters perform these unaccustomed labours, from time to time bringing them cooling drinks or, in some cases, playing records on gramophones which they had transported to the site. It was a bizarre spectacle, authentically West African, and as far removed from the realities of World War II as it would be possible to imagine.

To my great delight I was posted, on completing this course, to Kano in Hausa country, in the same latitude as Sokoto, where the 12th Battalion of the Nigeria Regiment was in process of formation, though so far it existed only on paper. 'I look forward to being here for a fairly long stretch,' I wrote, 'and have sent a voluminous telegram to Williams, a D.O. whom I knew in Sokoto, enquiring about a horse I have heard of.' In the meanwhile our own training continued, as the first intake of recruits had not yet arrived, and during this period I was able to get away for a few days on my own again, up to the northern border, nominally on a reconnaisance, 'marvellous country, completely flat, with the horizon forming the complete circle, like coming out of a prison, after being in the south'. Here as dusk fell over the silent and treeless plain I experienced the same sense of contact with infinity and elevation of spirit that had come to me with such force on my first journey to Sokoto, and I felt it would be death to go back to the southern forests again. So in true Hausa fashion I got myself a charm, calling on the way home at the stalls of the money dealers in Kano market, who bought and sold every currency there was to be had in the northern half of Africa. It was a Maria Theresa dollar, the coin which, for no very certain reasons, had for the past two centuries been the common unit of exchange in Abyssinia and the countries fringing the Red Sea. With this in my pocket there was some reassurance that routine regimental life would not last for ever.

Colonial Postscript

Actually of course it had not yet begun. It was already nearly Christmas before the African recruits started to arrive – including a few whom I had enlisted during a previous incarnation at Ankpa – and there was a lot to be done before we could start training them.

My platoon went down to be fitted with boots this morning. In this, like everything, one has to start from scratch with a lecture on which boot goes on which leg, avoiding words like left and right which are apt to be forgotten; the left hand is the one that holds the rifle, the right that with which food is eaten. In spite of that there are plenty of mistakes when the time comes. Then an old soldier is called to give a demonstration of how to put socks on, and the device of putting one hand down as far as the heel and then turning the sock back on itself is considered highly ingenious! Still I saw something I'd never seen before, a man struggling to put on a boot over a foot with the heel of the sock upwards instead of underneath. I shall be very glad when they have boots since although in their natural state their feet are pretty hard they follow paths instead of being led through thorns and rocks as they are now. Also the Harmattan which cracks our lips seems to play havoc with the soles of their feet and boots would give a lot of protection. They're rather like a lot of junior prep school boys, they love rather disorganized games with a lot of leaping about and shouting and calling of nicknames. They're very competitive and imitative and pick up quite complicated movements with extraordinary facility though without much understanding, that is especially so with things like arms drill where their natural instinct helps them to follow the rhythm much more easily than the English soldier would. Competent people say that after some training their drill is not excelled by anyone, even the regiments which specialize in it at home.

Besides teaching the recruits drill I was teaching Hausa to the British officers and N.C.O.s who had newly arrived in the country. The latter were

Northern Nigeria – Kano – RWAFF, 1940–1

painfully slow, being used to learning things parrot-wise first and only later (if at all) trying to understand them. The Regimental Sergeant Major who has been out here before tries to teach them to describe the movements of arms drill in Hausa phrases supposed to be the exact translation of the English, which of course they have by heart. So off they go to "punch up" (as their expression is) this completely meaningless mumbo-jumbo of sounds, and not only try but even succeed, which amazes me.

About this time my new horse arrived from Sokoto, and was named Lamarudu, the Hausa for Nimrod.

He cost me a lot of money – probably about £8 before I'm through [which was about a week's pay at the time] – which is quite high by local standards, but I've seldom had my legs over a more magnificent animal. He is a roan standing about the same height as Benjie, and he's pretty fast. His one defect is that he's frightened of the least trickle of water, like all horses from the Azben country, where there are only wells. . . Now I must admit I don't much mind how many months I do out here, and hope there'll be an Easter meeting again this year!

Horses were barred from the Kano township so I kept him

> in a small Fulani village just outside the boundary and in view from the house. If it weren't for the fact that we spend very little time here I should very likely have moved out there myself to get away from the crowd, as the Sarkin Fulani is a nice old gentleman and I am great pals with his children. I might even pick up some Fulani that way as they speak it among themselves, though they are all bilingual round here.

Nothing came of this plan as early in January 1941 I was sent off on home leave. It was a cold but fortunately uneventful journey in a wide sweep through the north Atlantic to avoid enemy submarines. On arrival I sought out the girl with whom I had exchanged so many letters, married her and lived happily ever after. But that is another story. We did not have long together before I was shipped off to West Africa again. But before going there I had spent a night in my old college at Cambridge and, over the port at high table, asked Kenneth Pickthorn who knew everybody and had been a pilot in World War I if he could get me transferred to the Royal Air Force. No, that was impossible, he said, but he asked me about West Africa and I must have mentioned Dan Fulani who, before he came to me, had accompanied Lord Rennel of Rodd during his travels through the Southern Sahara. Rennel, K.P. said, was even now setting up a military administration for the former Italian colonies in East Africa – Eritrea, Abyssinia and Somaliland, and he gave me an address in the War Office to visit. After an abortive visit to the Air Ministry I called on them, but there was little they could say, though they made a note of my name.

A few weeks later I was back in Kano again writing home to my mother.

I don't know whether the Ston Easton Women's Institute has done anything in the way of collecting "comforts" for the troops but if so it might amuse them to hear what we have got out of it at this end. We are very short of papers and magazines and there is never anything to read in the mess, so when I arrived there for breakfast this morning and found a pile of new ones I was rather pleased. But it was a bit of a shock to find that they consisted entirely – except for one copy of the Auckland N.Z. *Weekly Times* dated April 1933 – of *Woman's Own*, *Woman and Home*, *Woman's Friend* etc., all between four and five years old. Someone I fear has been getting mixed up between the initials of the West African Frontier Force and the Women's Auxiliary Air Force. But you know how it is, people will read anything rather than nothing and there we were sitting round the table, diligently absorbing articles on how to feed baby or choose spring curtains or extremely glutinous serial stories from the various journals

Northern Nigeria – Kano – RWAFF, 1940–1

propped up in front of us. Thank you, Comforts for the Forces!

The extract just quoted is one of the few lighter spots in letters which reflect the tedium of army life in Northern Nigeria at the time. For a short while, it is true, the two Kano battalions had been alerted to move up to the border. 'It was a real scare and not an artificial one, so we had all the preparation for going off on an expedition. We've been standing to at an hour's notice ever since,' I wrote, 'but I'm convinced that nothing will happen, as it's so completely opposed to the interests either of ourselves or of the French that trouble should start in this part of the world.' During my leave there had been many changes, and most of my friends had been transferred to other more interesting jobs and their places taken by British officers from home to whom Nigeria was an unfortunate posting and the African soldiers so many indistinguishable black men. Indeed, the troops were not much to boast about, as those of them with personalities or intelligence were quickly picked out to provide N.C.O.s for other battalions. We had an extremely unpopular commanding officer who never knew what a risk he ran of being quietly deposited in a river on some moonless night. For a month or two in the middle of the rains we were occupied several times a week with army manœuvres, the confusion of which was nothing uncommon, I suppose, but gave us little confidence in our leader. 'This will be the second scheme,' I wrote,

> Wednesday night we also spent in bush up the road to . . . but that I may not tell you. Anyway it was 50 miles or so from here in a district which I had not visited before, where there was a patch of thickish bush, unlike the open farmland which extends for miles round this city in all directions. Here we were to practise movement in country similar to that which we would be likely to find in the sparsely inhabited parts of East Africa (where we still imagined that we might be sent, if the fighting was not over before we arrived) and as we also had an enemy and a night out the scheme included the forming

Colonial Postscript

of a camp and a battle on the second day. We had a quiet night fortunately and no rain or attacks from the "enemy"; there was a terrific outcry from the platoon next door which made us think that the enemy was upon us, due, it turned out, to a sleeping soldier being sniffed at and scratched by a passing hyena. I saw him the next day with his leg bandaged looking very pleased with himself – the only casualty of the war!

Soon afterwards we finished battalion training for the year and split up again into companies and platoons to carry out the basic arms drill and musketry training which had been left incomplete in the previous year because of the emergency. This was extremely boring, although the close daily contact with the African troops revealed many unknown aspects of their character and caused one again and again to marvel at their patience and ingenuity. They saw life in direct and homely terms and as always the language was a key to their thoughts. Among themselves the trigger of the rifle was the 'scorpion' because of its curly tail, the butt was the 'backside', and there were other nicknames even more indelicate. Some of the N.C.O.s began to realise how much more quickly they could 'get across' when they adopted this kind of approach, and from that moment my job as language instructor to the battalion became easier, and gave me time for my own studies . . .

> partly with an eye to my own future – some day – and partly for the fun of it I've started working with a mallam three times a week, who teaches me Arabic through the medium of Hausa, so I shall improve my knowledge of the latter even if I don't make much progress in the former. Since Aden days I've kept two elementary readers used by little Egyptian boys in their first six months at school, on which I'm beginning now. I thought that parts of them were unduly difficult until I discovered that in conscientiously setting out to read the thing through from the first page to the last, or rather from the last page to the first, I was trying to cope with the footnotes or

Northern Nigeria – Kano – RWAFF, 1940–1

instructions to the teacher as well. How long our own programme of work will permit me to arrange with someone to come and give me regular teaching I don't know, but I think I may get two or three months of it.

Lamarudu had been rather a disappointment since he was always going lame but some of my best hours were still those spent with him.

I went out for a ride this evening and saw a most magnificent storm breaking over the city, like the scene in the *Freischutz* which I saw in Leipzig (only not quite so brilliant perhaps because the German producer would inevitably try to outdo nature). Fortunately none of the flashes came very near, or my horse would have been off to bush and sent me for a six. The local electric lighting plant is very vulnerable because it always seems to get blown out when there is a storm ... I wish I could describe the storms to you, pitch-black skies which turn the colour of the trees into a dark and almost purple green, forked lightning not in rare flashes but almost continuous enough to read the paper by and rain when it arrives so torrential that you can see the road surface being washed off and carried away before your eyes.

The last storms of the rainy season, always the most intense, were followed by a period of sticky heat excellent for ripening the millet and the Guinea corn but hard on the troops doing their drill on an open parade ground. After a scorching morning one was glad to get back to the shade of the mess at lunchtime. But one day instead of lunch there was a message to report at once to the Orderly Room. This was also the Adjutant's office, and there was the Adjutant, a little-loved man with a strong temper, the state of which could be gauged from the colour of a carbuncle on his neck. Saluting, I noticed that today it was very, very red. He was holding an open telegram. 'What have you been up to?' he roared. Naturally, I affected complete ignorance,

Colonial Postscript

but I could guess what it contained and my heart leapt with a great hope. It was better even than expected. Second Lieutenant Morley was to report at once to East Africa Command, and to be accorded number one priority in getting there. And this, the Adjutant explained with rising indignation, meant that Brigadier X. would have to step down so that I could take his seat. It seemed time for me to say something and I enquired when the flight left – at 6 a.m. tomorrow.

Flying across Africa was a leisurely business in those days with plenty of stops. At one of these General de Gaulle – only I think he was a Colonel then – joined the plane; no doubt he had been to inspect the Free French force which was about to launch an attack on the Fezzan. At Khartoum we transferred to one of the old Imperial Airways flying boats which flew along the Nile, and at Kisumu to another aircraft for the final stage through Kenya. A week after leaving Kano I was in the bar of the Norfolk Hotel, Nairobi, digging in my pockets for some change. Out came the Maria Theresa dollar, which I presented forthwith to a complete stranger standing next to me, explaining to her that it was a very powerful fetish, which had now done its work as far as I was concerned.

IX
Eritrea – Massawa, 1941–2

Already by May 1941, only eleven months after the Italian declaration of war, the Allied forces (which included a Gold Coast contingent but none from Nigeria) had occupied all her East African empire – Eritrea, the three Somalilands and the whole of Abyssinia except for the isolated fortress of Gondar in the northwest. Lord Rennel, who was charged with the task of setting up a military admistration over these thousands of square miles of territory, says in his history that he searched in vain for precedents and principles in the War Office archives, but concluded that the British planning staff had never envisaged a conquest and occupation of enemy territory! The speed of the advance had also taken everyone by surprise. 'The headquarters of O.E.T.A. (Occupied Enemy Territory Administration),' I wrote in my first letter from Nairobi,

> remind me of an unusually small hedgesparrow trying to cope with five outsize cuckoos which have been unexpectedly desposited in its nest. Ever since the day when the young birds grew with alarming speed to their present size the wretched foster mother has been hard pressed to supply the requisite number of worms in the shape of men, money and organization that her various step children demand.

I also learnt more about my own case and

> gather from one who has seen my personal file here that the haste with which I was summoned wasn't due to a suddenly

Colonial Postscript

reached decision but resulted from an exchange of cables that has been going on for some time, with West Africa maintaining a Pharoah-like attitude throughout, and the Colonial Office acting as Moses I presume.

My choice would have been to go to Abyssinia, with which there had been such close connections in the days of Besse. Moreover I had once met Haile Selassie during his exile in England, 'on his way from Bath to London, in a third class railway carriage. To travel in a third class railway carriage and still look like an Emperor takes some doing, but H.S. managed it'. On the last stage of the journey across Africa, from Kisumu to Nairobi, I mentioned these hopes to a friendly brigadier sharing the same aircraft, discovering too late that he was Kennedy-Cooke, the newly appointed Chief Political Officer in Eritrea. Shortly afterwards I heard that it was to Eritrea that I was to be posted, which was a matter for regret at the time but turned out to be a very fortunate coincidence.

It was quite a long way by sea from Mombasa to Massawa, in a troopship which, even at that stage of the war, had already begun quite literally to crack up – on the last day of the voyage 'a large piece of reinforcement crashed from the bridge onto the crowded deck below'. No-one was killed, fortunately, but two of the Somali crew were seriously injured. Besides this we were short of water and the cabins so full of vermin that my companion confessed he would be disappointed if we did not see a snake before the voyage was complete. He had a complete set of Linguaphone records, and we set ourselves a crash course in learning Italian by this highly effective method. 'I've dropped Arabic for the time being,' I wrote from on board

> and spend most of the day listening to the adventures of the family Lebrun, their friends Signor Bernardi and Signor Durante, the children Nella, Carlo, Lilla and the bambino who doesn't appear to have been christened yet. Signor Lebrun is the owner of a house in a Milan suburb which he takes one of his loathsomely servile friends to visit, from

Eritrea – Massawa, 1941–2

whose half-witted econiums one might imagine that they were inspecting a palace.

I was soon to find that in Eritrea as in Italy any building of more than ordinary style was a 'palazzo' or at least a 'palazzina'. My appointment was to be that of Civil Affairs Officer, equivalent to an Assistant District Officer, with the rank of lieutenant, since this was a military, not a civil administration.

Massawa is not an easy port to enter at the best of times and the harbour was now full of sunken ships. 'As we approached there were a number of explosions, not that we were close enough to hear anything, but we could watch one pillar of smoke arising and another quickly following, until whatever it was had finished and the cloud dispersed again.' There was

> a succession of hills running parallel to the shore in tiers, with the last quite impressively high. It was a larger place than I had somehow expected, with a number of dock-like buildings and a large two-storeyed house on the point over which it was gratifying to see the Union Jack flying.

This was the Governor-general's palace – a real palace if only a small one – constructed of dazzlingly-white coral, which is sufficiently soft when first lifted out of the sea to be sawn into blocks. It was not a permanent vice-regal residence, having been used only for a month or two in the winter, when the climate of Massawa is quite agreeable. Its present occupant was the Senior Political Officer, Bassopiano Orientale, who had characteristically asserted the predominance of the civil arm of the administration by snatching the principal residence in the town from under the nose of the military commander the moment it had fallen into British hands – an act for which the military never quite forgave him. My cabin companion and I, and one or two others who were joining O.E.T.A. had lunch with him in the sweltering heat of the port before proceeding on our way to report to headquarters at Asmara, up the hill at a height of nearly 8000 feet and always cool, sometimes even cold. How-

Colonial Postscript

ever, my first letter after landing in Eritrea reports, I had 'instantly decided that he [Col. Miller] was the type of man one would surrender a great many advantages of climate to be able to work with', and headquarters lost no time in returning me to him. There were no other volunteers.

It was a good choice though it didn't seem so at first. Twelve months later when I was still in the same Division but by then in charge of it I wrote:

> the Brigadier's Personal Assistant said when they were down here a week ago that this place had double, treble the fascination of Asmara ... I remember vividly arriving down here on a sticky evening and being whisked along most unwillingly to a drinks party at the hotel. And then going over to the office in the morning and being handed the first file – it dealt with trade, I remember – and gazing at it with the blank despair that comes over one (I've seen it come over others) when stepping into unfamiliar surroundings. The only thing experience teaches is that even the most heartbreakingly strange will become one day familiar, and that one will be very, very lucky if one can find people ready to spare the time to explain things.

There was not much explaining that could be done in Massawa, where the administration was only just beginning to function again after the surrender, and law and order were still far from being established. The explosions we had seen from the ship were the tail end of a gigantic fire which had swept the vast civil and military base depot maintained by the Italians in the port, destroying huge quanitites of food, equipment, fuel, tyres and all the things that could have been used to put the colony on its feet again. When it occurred, there were no fire-fighting appliances to protect it and, now that the base was gutted, there was no police force to keep out the looters. Indeed the Sudan Defence Force were at one time looting it themselves, and almost fought a pitched battle among its ruins. Gradually order was restored, and large numbers of Eritrean natives who had joined in were

Eritrea – Massawa, 1941–2

sent across to the civil court which had been hurriedly established. Here Colonel Miller, who knew no Italian (the language in which the court had to function), and who in any case had other things to do than run a court had, prior to my arrival, been disposing of some 50/60 cases in a morning, issuing sentences ranging from six months in prison to 12 strokes with the cane; he explained to me, with a twinkle in his own eyes, that he could see from the look in theirs whether they were guilty of the offence with which they had been charged! Being unable to perform these miracles of instant justice and with a fair part of the criminal population effectively discouraged by this time, I reduced the flow of cases by about nine-tenths but, even so, struggling with the Italian of Signor Lebrun, must have punished as large a proportion of the innocent, and discharged as many of the guilty, as Bill Miller had done by the old method.

While Miller spoke no Italian he was a splendid Arab linguist, which gave him great prestige with the native population of the Sahel, the coastal strip of Eritrea and its adjacent islands with a mixed but mainly Arabic-speaking population. It also meant that, while not one of them, he had to be taken seriously by the 'heaven-born' of the Sudan Political Service, several of whose officers held high positions in the military administration and were a little inclined to treat Eritrea as the Sudanese protectorate which many expected it would one day become. To a run-of-the-mill colonial administrator the Sudan, with its special status under the Foreign Office and its special civil service ('blues ruling the blacks', they were sometimes described), were objects of admiration and also some wonder; I recall with particular delight my first encounter with one of them who was complaining to a colleague about the Italian veterinary officer. 'My dear chap, he speaks no known language,' meaning of course that he could converse in neither Arabic nor English. Miller not only passed this test but he had the further almost unique experience of having served in the earlier military administration of Palestine in World War I under Allenby. This had impressed upon him the importance of rapid decisions, which he proceeded to impress upon me. In these early days ships arrived without

Colonial Postscript

warning in Massawa with all sorts of problems aboard, like the thousands of Eritrean and Ethiopian prisoners of war from other parts of the front, on whom we wasted no time in finding them temporary accommodation and still less in reporting their presence or asking for instructions, but chartered immediate transport to their homes or as near to them as could be arranged, with a grant of 50 lire each for food on the journey. Better a number of small problems throughout the country, he rightly thought, than one big one in Massawa! It was surprising to find how many officers had great difficulty in coming to the quick decisions that such occasions required; I remember one of them, a distinguished member of the Bar in private life, confessing how foreign it was to his nature to arrive at decisions without first sifting all the facts and examining all the precedents. In Massawa facts were often difficult to determine, and precedents did not exist.

As the months passed and the tide of war ebbed to more distant fronts, the naval and military garrisons in Eritrea were scaled down, while our own responsibilities daily increased. The prison, the hospitals, the post and telegraph department, the customs service, the port authority had to be taken over or recreated and put into some sort of shape which would satisfy the military requirements, as well as conventional colonial ideas about how such services should operate and the capacities of those who could be found to run them. There was plenty of scope for experiment and no lack of experimenters – Polish doctors who could speak no English, university specialists in obscure subjects who had been posted by the War Office to an area where it was felt they could do no harm, a fair number of misfits from the forces who, as a rule, fitted equally badly into their new surroundings, together with a handful of colonial administrators from all parts of Africa and the Middle East combined to make O.E.T.A. – 'Open Every Thursday Afternoon', its detractors called it – a most interesting and stimulating organization to be in. The machinery creaked and groaned and operated at a low level of efficiency; it would hardly have worked at all without the participation of a large number of

Eritrea – Massawa, 1941–2

Italians who, with the bribe of a ration card and an undertaking not to look too deeply into past misbehaviour, were for the most part only too glad to collaborate. These were not the higher rank of policy-makers, whom it was thought safer in most cases to intern, but the lower grade of Government employee; policemen, mechanics, lorry drivers and the like, performing tasks which in any British colony would have been carried out entirely by Africans. One of the facts that came to light very early on was that for all the hundreds of British who had learnt some French, or German, or Spanish at school there were hardly any who had knowledge of Italian. We overcame this difficulty fairly soon, and in doing so became warmly attached to the Italian nation, and they to us I think; to such an extent that when later on there was an American 'invasion' of Eritrea, many of us found our 'allies' less congenial than those who, though technically our 'enemies' were citizens of the same continent and shared something of the same cultural background. They were resilient and adaptable, making use of the local Yemeni grapes and raisins to replace the Chianti that could no longer be imported, performing miracles of patching and refurbishing worn-out tyres and organizing a variety of local industries to help out with the semi-siege conditions. Many of them had come to Eritrea as employees of the contractors who had built the great monument to Italian rule in East Africa, the superb trunk road system which, starting in Massawa, crossed the coastal plain, climbed effortlessly up the escarpment to Asmara at the top, and then went down through the Keren gorge to the Bassopiano Occidentale, or Western Plain. Other links had been driven south into Abyssinia, to Axum, to Gondar where the last battle had been fought, and to Addis Ababa. 'Credere, obbedire, combattere', shouted the slogans on the parapets of the bridges; 'Believe, Obey, Fight', and 'Mussolini ha sempre ragione', 'Mussolini is always right.' The Italians averted their eyes as they drove us past. Overhead and crossing the road from time to time ran the *Teleferica*, said to be the longest cable-way in the world, which had been built for transporting stores from the coast to the main forward base at Asmara, but the baboons had learnt how to rob the conveyors and it was more often at a standstill than working. Alongside the road, sometimes high above and sometimes below it, driving through mountain spurs and cornering precipices, ran the third artery of the railway, which the road had now supplanted though a diesel car still made the journey up and down twice a day. 'I have been taking a new arrival in the Asmara secretariat for a conducted tour,' I wrote one week, after the summer heat had begun again, and visitors from the Altopiano were rare,

> he had come down by train to look at the place and being a conscientious person and not really travelling on duty he had insisted on paying for his ticket. Such a thing is all but unknown on the Eritrean railways and caused consternation because the tickets were kept in a box which hadn't been opened for such a long time that they had mislaid the key!

This officer will reappear in the story as he and I and one other formed a small mess in Asmara some months later, but that comes in the next chapter.

Mail between Eritrea and England was very irregular, being often held up for a week or so if any important military moves were in progress, in case any information about them should get into the wrong hands. Anyone wanting to communicate in a hurry had to use the 'forces' telegram' system, which allowed him or her to pick any three out of a list of some 50 stereotyped phrases covering birth, death, bereavement, state of health and so on. The system made individual self-expression pretty difficult, except that one could, by a combination of phrases, sometimes achieve a sense of meaning other than the inventor of the system had intended – thus '32 – 32 – 32' (assuming that to have been the number) stood for 'well! well! well!', though without the exclamation marks, of course. Another device was the aerogram, consisting of a square piece of paper on which the solider wrote his message, with a space at the top for the address. This was photographed on microfilm and enlarged again to approximately post card size when it got back to

Eritrea – Massawa, 1941–2

England; but the messages were often barely legible and aerograms were not popular with those at home.

Only about half the letters have survived which I sent to my mother from Massawa – and none at all after that – and these the less interesting ones, the others having no doubt been sent by her on a circular tour round the family from which they never returned. Most of those that are left describe the fairly ordinary doings of life in Massawa and here chosen almost at random is one dated 29 January 1942, just ten days after my elder daughter had been born. (I recall being congratulated on the event in elegant Arabic by the Naib, the paramount chief in the Massawa area.)

The President of the Sessions court, which has had its opening sitting down here, and the Prosecutor have been staying here the last few days. They are in rather a curious position as both of them were involved in a row in Asmara over Christmas as a result of which, justly or unjustly, they have been forbidden to go to any place of public resort or entertainment for the following two months. Rather an odd situation in which two leading members of the judicial department should find themselves! As usual I can't tell you very much about what has been going on here, except that there has been plenty. I don't know that the work has actually increased, but it has got to the point where I often spend days without seeing the Colonel or having more than a brief telephone chat with him, even though we're in the same office. A new officer has come down to take over the Finance side of things – we have successively 'shed' Police, Commercial, Enemy Property, P.W.D., Customs and Financial matters and devoted ourselves to the more definitely political functions – only Medical remains to be dropped and it will be a very good thing when we have an English doctor to control the host of Italian doctors and wardens and nurses, who frig about most of the time, it seems to me, and write us, or one another, letters without getting down to the job. The astonishing thing is that there is no less left after all these 'sheddings' for us to do – or

Colonial Postscript

perhaps it gets done more thoroughly – and even more surprising, a month after one of the new departments gets going, its affairs, which took up a hectic ten minutes of one's time before, seem to keep quite busily employed an officer, whole time, with two or three clerks of his own. To create staff is in fact to create work at almost the same rate, and the Italians carried this to such a degree that they would have a staff of ten in a one-man office before you could say Presto! (presumably what an Italian would say!), and then have to bring in an eleventh and call him the officer in charge of office personnel, who would have the biggest job of the lot.

Despite these preoccupations in Massawa itself I soon found

> an excuse to visit some small villages up the coast and make some sort of apology for conversation with the Sheikhs who entertain you here to cups of coffee, a form of hospitality which unfortunately didn't exist over the other side (of Africa). One I visited this morning was said by my driver, whom I took with me, to be the greatest chief in Eritrea; perhaps this was because he came of the same house. The village was of no great size and the buildings, except for a mosque of stone, all constructed from grass. The chief seized me firmly by the hand and led me around as though I were a small boy, not letting me go until he had me seated on the carpet (a very nice one, though I thought I'd better not say so in case courtesy compelled him to give it to me). The Yemenis to whom these Arabs are closely akin are very fond of going about holding hands but I hadn't known before that they did the same to Europeans . . . It is all, as one would expect, barren enough, just sand and pebbles with an occasional thorn tree, and sometimes a wadi bed, so broad and flattened out that it would not be recognizable except that the same dark shrub which grows so freely in the desert behind Aden is here too, and confines vehicles to a single track where the sand is often much less firm than it appears and you find yourself changing down all the gears in less time than it takes

Eritrea – Massawa, 1941–2

to write this, in order to avoid becoming bogged ... At one point there is a little cultivation of the ultra-hardy millet which grows here and in the Yemen; the fields are surrounded by walls of earth, I suppose to prevent the shortlived spate from the mountains being wasted, and of course they are built across the road too, so it is bump, bump as you go over with a sickening interval between when you wonder whether the middle of the car is going to scrape half way over.

At another village there was a fete

in honour of a Moslem saint whose mortal remains are supposed to be buried there, and who is the ancestor of the present Sheikh of the village, a pious, plausible, dirty old rogue who is held in high repute and is believed to have the power of intercession which is not accorded to many. He is probably the most reputable 'saint' in Eritrea, but fortunately does not intervene in politics, at any rate directly. Yesterday afternoon he was certainly cashing in on his reputation, since entrance to the shrine cost ten lire a nob and at least a thousand people must have been present on the pilgrimage, including deputations and processions carrying flags from all the main villages hereabouts. Very colourful, against the green and yellow background (the desert still being green after the rains), the Yemenis in particular favour a bright head-dress, and there were women of the Rashaida tribe heavily veiled and wearing thick head-dresses most elaborately embroidered with silver threads and shells and coins. Outside the tomb practically every gambling game known to the Arab world must have been in full swing. The saint disapproved but considered honour satisfied when the the thing was officially forbidden; a native *askari* with a fine show of officiousness followed us around and upset the gambling tables as we approached – but we told him to desist as however excellent the intention (and however momentary the results!) I have always disliked fostering the idea that Europeans are so foolish as to be taken in by such pretended devotion to duty.

He knows that he will stop as soon as your back is turned, you know it too, but does he know that you know? It is important not to leave the matter in any doubt.

'As usual I'm snowed under with work,' another letter begins,

and have some tricky things tomorrow (Sunday) which will keep me in the office for the morning at any rate. Can't be helped! I've just had two days away and enjoyed them immensely, dealing finally (I hope) with a land dispute which has been going on intermittently since 1934 and whose origins date back considerably further. The Colonel was to have gone and I had everything laid on and ready for him when he rang over to say that he didn't see a possibility of leaving himself so would I like to go instead? I didn't give him a chance to change his mind. *And* sat up until well after midnight so as to clear the office table, and got away the next day without even forgetting the tin-opener and the toilet paper, the two things that I find always get left behind! .... The story is not untypical of land disputes, and it may interest you to hear it. Down here in what they call the Bassopiano Orientale there are two types of cultivation, that which is planted in the hopes of rain and an occasional flood and that which is grown in a properly irrigated system of banks and dykes. The people who carry on the latter type have a much greater interest in the soil than those who merely take a crop off it where they can and when they can. To start with, they have to be there not only in the rains, but in the hot dry season as well, in order to repair the dykes and make more of them. The estuary at this place is one of those where the floodwater can be 'tapped' without too much difficulty, i.e. the banks are not at all high, and there would be natural flooding anyway, which is not too difficult to control. A tribe called the Aflenda Nasr-ed-Din carries on a moderately elaborate cultivation in this manner, but between 1934 and 1938 another tribe called the Ad Derchi, who were immigrants in this part of the world, came and cultivated it too in a somewhat half-hearted manner,

Eritrea – Massawa, 1941–2

that's to say they built one dyke and that not a very long one. Then they discovered another place about 20 miles away where they could use the flood waters to their advantage, and made a very good thing out of them. Since 1938 I believe they have not sown any crops in the estuary at all, nevertheless being a litigious people they kept their claim alive and pretended the only reason why they had not cultivated there was because of the *force majeure* of the Aflenda. Except for a few areas of which this is one, Italian land law recognizes no form of property except the state or its concessionaires, consequently it is necessary to show that you are in effective occupation of the soil to get a *de facto* recognition of your right to remain there.

I've forgotten all the details of how this case eventually reached the governor of the colony for him to give his fiat. The dispute had been quite fairly reported but for political reasons it was decided to favour the Ad Derchi who really hadn't a leg to stand on. However the Ad Derchi are slightly holy, and Musso was in one of his Protector of Islam moods. So the land was divided between them just before the war, probably in a somewhat inefficient manner. The Aflenda were very upset, and profited from the general disturbance of the war and the impermanent nature of whatever boundary marks had been put up to take them all down again. More wails from the Ad Derchi who could now adopt a righteous attitude of those who would bring law-breakers to justice. This was the situation shorn of its trimmings (and there is nothing so richly adorned with red herrings as a land case). I decided that it was quite unnecessary for the Ad Derchi to have any land at all. But the position in international law about what changes you can make in the legal decisions of an occupied enemy territory and what you can't touch is not at all simple, and Colonel Miller was of the opinion that justice could be done without any reversal of the previous decision by giving the better half to the Aflenda and the worse to the Ad Derchi. Just when I was wondering what I could use to make permanent and visible boundary posts I came across the very thing I wanted, some iron traffic-parking signs in an abandoned road construction company's yard. So I took them up there with me, and sunk them in cement. They are in line, so it will be very easy to see if any of them get moved. (The locals were not told about this, of course.) And it affords me very considerable satisfaction to think that in ten or 20 years time, when the river has changed its course and the posts still stand on the banks of a wadi down which water never flows, someone will come along and wonder how three 'Halt' signs ever found their way into that particular wilderness'.

'On the way back I ran into some Rashaida. These are the Ishmaelites of Eritrea; whenever you come to a particularly desolate piece of country, up pops a Rashaida youth of ten years or under leading a camel. They are fairer-skinned than our local coastal 'Arabs' who have got too mixed up with the local stock to deserve that designation really. They are I believe fairly recent immigrants, and in small groups of families they cover a vast area, not only in Eritrea but in the Sudan. I told him that it wouldn't surprise me to find some of his tribesmen in England. 'Certainly,' he said, being quite unable to conceive a world without Rashaida in it.

The only general map of Eritrea that we had available at that time has scrawled across it the names of various tribes – Ad Sheikh, Habab, Ad Tumariam and many others – in the regions where they were supposed to wander. These tribes were relics of larger communities which had been unsuccessful in the battle for life, or perhaps merely unlucky, and had been pushed out of the more fertile areas into the tangle of wild and inhospitable mountains facing a barren shore which make up the northern part of Eritrea, where there are no permanent settlements because there are no permanent pastures or water supplies through which life can be sustained. So there was an annual pattern of movement, of the tribes coming down out of the mountains in the autumn, and returning there when the stock of grass left by the brief winter rains had become exhausted. There was a little cultivation on the plateau, but this depended on local

Eritrea – Massawa, 1941-2

rainfall which was very uncertain. Further south, the division of climate was quite clearly marked; indeed there was a point just outside Asmara on the Massawa road where it could be narrowed down to the space of a hundred yards, on one side of which rain fell only in January and February, and on the other between June and August. Here in the north the rains were much less reliable and in some seasons little fell at all. Altogether I made three trips into various parts of this savage but interesting country, where it did not take long to find that the maps were speculative and approximate not only as to the whereabouts of the tribes but also as to the situation of mountains and valleys; very often therefore we would impress an unwilling tribesman to accompany us for part of the way, paying him for his services in the only acceptable currency, a few handfuls of the dried dates with some raisins which we kept in a sack and on which we also fed ourselves. The object of the first journey was to make an inspection of the emergency landing ground at Mersa Teclei, up in the extreme north, since there were some fears that enemy aircraft might sow magnetic mines in the northern channel to the port of Massawa, and as the islands and coastline on both sides of this channel were uninhabited some aerial patrol of the region might be necessary. The place when we found it was utterly deserted, but on the way back we overtook a caravan of Habab tribesmen on the move, their camels laden with poles and other paraphernalia of their tents, and decorated with nodding ostrich plumes dyed scarlet – it made a brave and unusual sight. The journey along the coast had been difficult and somewhat hazardous, so on the return journey I followed a different route through the mountains, which led me past Keren and introduced me for the first time to Ken Trevaskis, a famous Eritrean character who will reappaear at a later stage in this narrative.

'A few days ago I had a most interesting experience,' I wrote a little later from Massawa.

I was informed by a native that he could lead me to hidden treasure. I took him and a British policeman to a spot about

Colonial Postscript

50 miles from here, expecting to find the usual mare's nest, and was still more unbelieving when instead of his leading me to a building, the guide took me to a sort of rubbish dump on the side of a hill, where he insisted we should find the concealed stuff. So we dug for an hour or two on top of the dump finding nothing, but the guide was still sure, while the local Italians who said they knew nothing looked somewhat uneasy. So I sent for more labourers with picks and shovels to start digging at the other end, and after removing all the usual empty tins and bottles at last we heard the welcome sound of iron on concrete. Everyone worked then with a will and soon we had uncovered a broad concrete slab, which proved to be the lintel of a doorway. Another half hour and we had uncovered enough to make a hole through the door, climb through and go down a short passage into a room where stacks and stacks of the 'stuff' (how I wish I could tell you what it was!) was piled. I left the policeman to get the doorway cleared, got into my car and raced 15 miles to the nearest phone. A lorry with soldiers was sent and we got half of it away that evening, and took the remainder next day. It was so heavy that loading it onto the lorry took many hours. It will be of the utmost value to us, in fact it is perhaps the most important of the finds which have been made in occupied enemy territory.

The last sentence may have been an exaggeration! My mother was most curious to know what this 'treasure' consisted of and rather disappointed to be told after the war that what had been buried was the lighting equipment and machinery for the lighthouses all the way down the Red Sea coast, which the Italians had presumably dismantled at the outbreak of hostilities and hidden so that we should not find it when the fighting was over. Nevertheless the discovery was important, as about this time we were having to give more attention to maritime affairs. On top of the scare about magnetic mines in the northern approaches had come another disturbing episode.

This involved, of all unexpected people, the Hausa community

Eritrea – Massawa, 1941–2

in Massawa, known locally as Takruri. In an earlier chapter I explained how these folk came to be here, on their way to Mecca, after walking 3000 miles across Africa. Now, having got this far, almost within sight of their goal, they could get no further. In the first place all emigration was strictly controlled – there was an Italian mission still active in the Yemen, on the opposite coast, which was almost certainly in illicit contact with underground patriot leaders in Eritrea. Secondly the authorities in the Hejaz, where the holy cities lay, were far from eager to admit them. West African pilgrims tended to be the poor relations of Islam, and in a normal year they performed a useful service, undertaking the menial tasks for which there was always a need in the pilgrim season. Now however the pilgrimage was virtually at a standstill, because of the war, and King Ibn Saud wanted to get rid of the Africans he already had, not to add to their number. 'Every now and then a dhow arrives with Nigerian pilgrims stranded in Mecca for the past two or three years,' I wrote,

> and usually not permitted to land here by the Port Police who want to send them to Suakim. So far I have always persuaded them to turn a blind eye, saying that they are British Protected Persons and should therefore be 'afforded every assistance and protection of which they may stand in need', as the passport has it, but really because I feel very paternal towards these children far from their homes, despised by the Arabs and just so many more black men to the Europeans. Here they don't put their best face on the world, since the village where they and the Sudanese colony live is supposed to harbour most of the thieves in the town – I think that in the course of their journey they fall into the habit of accepting contributions from the villages they pass before these have actually been offered them!

Naturally these Hausa, when they had recovered from their surprise at finding a European who could speak their language, turned to me as the one who could solve their problems. Surely

Colonial Postscript

I could, if I would, produce for them a *takarda*, the magic piece of paper which would open all doors, the door out of Eritrea, the door into the Holy Cities. But of course I was not able to do this, and could only urge them to patience. They listened to my advice but some of them did not follow it. A large group of them approached a dhow owner, who agreed for a big sum of money, paid in advance, to smuggle them out of the country and into the Hejaz but, he said, the landing must be made in an out of the way place and in darkness, lest they all be discovered and turned back or imprisoned. So it was settled, and off they went. At dead of night they were landed on a lonely shore, but when the day dawned and the dhow had gone they found they had been marooned on an uninhabited island, where they all died of thirst except for one man who by some miracle escaped and returned to Massawa to tell the tale.

The islands of the Dahlak archipelago – there were at least a hundred of them though only two or three were inhabited – formed part of our Commissariato but were so low lying that they could not be seen from Massawa. My first proper view of them was when I chanced to be returning from Asmara by the old road quite early in the morning after a night's rain. I paused before turning down the open hillside, to take in the details of a view which I have never seen equalled before or since. Seven to eight thousand feet below lay the coastal plain like a map at my feet, on which I could pick out not only Archico bay, where Massawa was, 40 miles away, but also quite clearly the Buri peninsula and the outlines of the main Dahlak island, both of them 80 miles off, and even I thought, though I could not be sure of it, the glint of the sea beyond them a hundred miles from the point where I was standing. This main island which looked so beautiful sparkling in the sunlight had in fact a most evil reputation since it had been used as a detention camp for political prisoners, and conditions there out of the sight and sound of men were, as one might expect, indescribable. Colonel Miller's first administrative act – this was before my arrival – had been to go out and release all the wretches lying there, imprison their guards, and turn all the property over to the local

Eritrea – Massawa, 1941–2

Arab chief, one Sheikh Seraj, adjuring him with mighty oaths not to abuse his trust. Sheikh Seraj was not only a very competent man but a most agreeable one too, a seafaring Arab who delighted the Colonel with his tales of pearl fishing, and in particular his explanation of how the pearl finds its way into the oyster. This was by a drop of rain falling on a calm sea and not, as one might suppose, being mingled with salt water, but sliding intact down all the way to the ocean floor and, in rare cases, right into the jaws of an oyster which happened to have its mouth open at that particular moment. Sheikh Seraj was made responsible not only for the prison camp on the islands but also for the collection of custom duties there and it was on his fast sailing dhow, the *Bil Bil*, that I made my first trip one Sunday afternoon out to the islands.

The purpose of my visit was to see whether the wooden buildings of the former prison camp could be dismantled and brought over to the mainland to provide temporary accommodation for the use of the Americans when they arrived to set up their main workshop in Eritrea. Five minutes inspection convinced me that they were weathered beyond the possibility of further usefulness and I set out to enjoy what was left of my time before returning on the morrow. That night and the following morning left on me an impression of unusual vividness, mainly perhaps because of the utter contrast with the bustle of the life that I had briefly left behind me. The stone-walled room where my bed was laid out – I had brought no servant with me – was absolutely quiet and still. Even the nearby sea made no noise and, on the bare wooden table set between two open doors, the candle flame burned motionless. The silence was intense and immaculate and when, next morning, the stir of life began again, that too was uncomplicated, a single sound of a man hammering on a boat, a mile away perhaps, with a faint echo as it reverberated across a wide stretch of water. I stood in the sunlight of the doorway, looking for its origin, but could see no one; then I went down to the small jetty, where the water was deep and clear to 15 feet or more and orange, blue and

Colonial Postscript

rainbow fish with silky fins moved round as in an aquarium. I held my breath and dived to a great depth to join them.

Anyone reading this narrative might be excused for thinking that touring was a vital part of the political officer's duties, as it had been in Northern Nigeria, and was to be again in my next two posts. This was not so; the tribal areas of the Bassopiano Orientale were sparsely inhabited and of very little political or economic importance. All in all I suppose I spent fewer days on tour than months in Massawa, but those are the days at this distance in time best remembered. In May just before Colonel Miller went off on leave for five or six weeks there came a last chance to do some exploring, this time in the Danakil desert, a wedge shaped area whose northern tip lay not too far from Massawa to the south. This is an area which has never been fully subdued, either by the Abyssinians or the Italians, and there is no reason why it ever should be by other conquerors, since it is impossible to conceive of other people than the Danakil being able to survive there. Its chief claim to fame was the barbaric custom practised by the inhabitants of mutilating the prisoners taken in war – a custom which had so impressed East Africa Command in Nairobi that officers about to be posted to Eritrea were often addressed in a squeaky voice by way of a reminder of what might be in store for them! Our route on this occasion lay only on the fringe of the desert, but passed through an area of much geological interest, a depression well below sea level yielding the only product of the region in which the outside world had an interest, namely salt. Overcoming their strong dislike of the plains the Abyssinians used to descend from the highlands in the winter to buy this precious commodity which the local inhabitants, sheltering from the sun in igloos composed of salt, dug out for them. By the time we passed this way it was already late in the year and the trade had literally dried up. Never have I experienced such heat, which was of course still further intensified by the glare reflecting from the completely bare and dead white surroundings. On the western fringe of the desert we had a rendezvous with our camels and proceeded northwards with them, keeping a weather

Eritrea – Massawa, 1941–2

eye on the storm clouds massing over the plateau immediately above us. For while we, on the coastal plain, were not far into our dry season, a heavy fall of the rain which was now due in the mountains could produce a sudden spate which would descend with alarming speed. Some of the khors or river beds were a mile or so across and there were abundant horror stories of slow moving caravans which had been halfway across and become engulfed.

When Colonel Miller returned from leave he was posted elsewhere but as by that time I had been acting in his place for some while and as moreover the Red Sea summer was well and truly upon us I was confirmed in the appointment and at the same time given a higher rank in order that the political branch would not be too heavily outgunned by the military and naval commands with which it had to deal. The change in status also involved taking up residence in the palace which I have previously mentioned in general terms but can now describe in detail. It was as I have said a most elegant building, approached by a marble stairway leading to a central hall with four main rooms off it. Three of these were bedrooms, each with a bathroom recess, and each in a different style, one all black marble, one in fake Egyptian where all the furniture including the double bed was covered with hieroglyphics, and one at the back in a style best described as domestic Italian. Evenings were spent on the verandah while at night in the early part of the summer, we slept on the roof. Later it became too hot for this and we returned below, to sleep or try to do so lying directly under the ceiling fan whirling overhead. Even so one would wake in the middle of the night, drenched with sweat, and tumble into the bath, though this did little to cool one. One night in desperation having had a bath I lay down again under the fan without drying, and got lumbago for my foolishness. Towards dawn there would usually be a cooler breeze off the sea but half way through the morning this dropped away and it stoked up again. All of us in Massawa got prickly heat, some so badly that they had to be removed altogether. The leave ration was three days up the hill in each fortnight – though few of us were able to take it – and I can recall the exact spot on the road to Asmara, somewhere near the 4000-foot mark where, on the way up, the body ceased to ooze and where, on the way down, it started again. The process was so uncomfortable that it was almost better not to go.

But, while the British sweated in time-honoured style, the old order was changing. The Americans, who had decided to set up a big base repair workshop in Eritrea, did things in quite different style. Even the advance party had refrigerators and air condition sets for the prefabricated bungalows they brought with them. How glad I was when I saw these being landed that they had not been offered the barrack huts from Nocra prison!

At the height of the summer the Duke of Gloucester arrived on a visit to the Middle East which brought him to Massawa. Here he was entertained by the Naval Officer in charge to lunch, to which of course the representatives of the other services were invited. After this was over it was not quite clear what should be done with H.R.H. during the time until he was due to fly on for his next appointment, and N.O.I.C. suggested that he might like to see the Massawa sights, of which there was only one, and accordingly I found myself showing off a palace to a royal duke – real life can be stranger than fairy stories. The Duke was interested in the green bed with the hieroglyphics and predictably wanted to know what they stood for. This was a stock question – and there was of course a stock answer!

Many departmental heads never appeared in Massawa except in January or February, while others found that duty called them even during the summer heat. The next visitor was Brigadier Longrigg, the new Chief Civil Affairs Officer, whose previous service had been in the Middle East so he knew exactly what questions to ask. 'I think the visit was quite successful,' I wrote, 'though it was rather a relief to have it over, in a manner of speaking it's an interview lasting twenty-four hours during which one is examined on a wider variety of subjects than any wretched university undergraduate had to pretend knowledge of. It may be just my imagination,' I added in the same letter, 'but though it's still * * * hot it's not quite so hot as it has been.

Eritrea – Massawa, 1941–2

I can't tell you what a relief it is to think you have turned the corner of a Red Sea summer. And yet I wouldn't have missed it for anything'. Longrigg told me that my time in Massawa was nearly up and a month later I had heard what my next job was to be. 'I have still got one or two big matters on hand before I can go away,' I wrote in mid September 1942,

> one of them is the providing of an answer to the Secretariat circular on the ethnological survey of the country, with the answers to which, sent in by the different divisions, I am later to be entrusted! They want information on a lot of things, linguistic, ethnic and religious divisions, and the movements of nomadic tribes, all illustrated by maps (how one is going to map the arbitrary wandering of some hundreds of subgroups of Danakil herdsmen in search of pasturage over an area 300 miles long by 50 to a 150 miles broad in any comprehensible fashion defeats me at the moment! But it will not all be so difficult). It is of course quite fantastic that one colony such as Nigeria should have its administrative staff so pared away that refinements such as anthropological research have been forgotten years ago, and that O.E.T.A. Eritrea can afford to spare an officer for an indefinite period to do so! However I can reconcile my conscience to the thought by treating it as a holiday, which is evidently how other people regard it too, for three people have already told me that they would like to be allowed to join me in the same 'work'. My plan at the moment is to go round all the main centres first and make a rough general picture so far as the persons there can supply the information required, and then if I am still not wanted for anything else proceed to make some long tours through the more inaccessible regions such as the Sudan frontier and in Dancalia, to get information which I am sure will be represented only very inaccurately at district headquarters. I *am* looking forward to it.

X
Eritrea – Hamasien, 1942–3

When the European powers divided Africa among themselves towards the end of the nineteenth century, they did so without too much regard for ethnic divisions, of which in any case they would have been largely ignorant. Consequently many African peoples having a common ancestry of sharing the same traditions found themselves on opposite sides of one of these new boundaries, while others having no relationship with their neighbours, except perhaps a hostile one, were united under the same colonial administration. Initially, while the reins of government still hung fairly loosely, the existence of these boundaries had little impact on the people concerned, but when tighter disciplines began to be enforced the anomalies of the situation became apparent. Eritrea, which had been first proclaimed an Italian colony in 1890, was a prime example of these incongruities. Broadly speaking it consisted of three quite distinct areas. The first was that of the central highlands, occupied for the most part by settled agriculturists, closely resembling their neighbours in the Abyssinian province of Tigrai, and having the same cultural, social and Christian traditions. The second was the western plain mostly occupied by nomadic or semi-nomadic pastoralists, Beja tribesmen closely akin to those over the Sudan border, with a Moslem allegiance. The third area was the coastal plain, thinly peopled except for the ports of Massawa and Assab, which were economically dependent upon trade with the highland regions. Furthermore, Eritrea was a small country, poor in natural resources, which would have difficulty in surviving on its own. With such considerations in mind, many believed that, when the time came to decide the country's future, the arbitrary boundaries of the past would be redrawn so as to take account of the wishes of its inhabitants who, it was thought – wrongly as it turned out – would favour partition, with the western plain falling to the Sudan and the remainder joining Abyssinia, or Ethiopia, as it was now called. In these circumstances the appointment of an officer to carry out an ethnological investigation was perhaps not quite the luxury it appeared, and I must have unwittingly recommended myself for the post through having compiled a potted history of Eritrea, on which I had had some correspondence already with Brigadier Longrigg. At the time however it did not occur to me to speculate why the post had been created or why I had been chosen to fill it, my one concern being to go while the going was good. My doubts whether the job would last turned out to be justified, but at least I had one interesting trip before being recalled to more mundane employment.

First I made for Keren, this being the buffer state between the highland and the plain, the Ethiopian and the Sudanese, the Copt and the Muslim. This was the area where the main dialogue would arise at any future peace treaty; almost as important perhaps, this was where Ken Trevaskis was living now. Thanks to the excellent roads in the colony travelling from one divisional headquarters to another presented no problem and many of the younger generation of political officers got to know one another well and to meet fairly frequently, sometimes in Asmara but more often in Keren. Here in a rambling house surrounded by bougainvillea and casuarina, and whose terrace overlooked the small town below, lived Ken with his dogs and his ponies and his servants, with seldom less than a dozen guests who had dropped in for the weekend. It was an ideally African establishment where lunch did not appear until well on in the afternoon, but always did appear in time so that a game of polo could be played in the last hour before sunset. Then there would be drinks and dinner and endless shop; 'the last thing I remember hearing before falling asleep,' said a lady visitor, 'was Ken and John talking about native administration'.

Colonial Postscript

Ken stayed on in Eritrea long after I left and wrote a professional history of the military administration; but also continued much later in the Colonial Service and became a distinguished Governor of Aden. But at this time we were both feeling our way to discovering more about the most interesting people among whom we worked, his being the more settled and primarily agricultural communities, mine being the more nomadic and pastoral, but there was no clear-cut division between them and one problem merged into another. The difference had been that while in Massawa the tribal areas were a secondary concern in Keren they were of major importance, and of particular interest to me at the present time since they included a large part of the northern hills – the hills towards which I had seen the camel caravans moving up from the coastal plain at the beginning of the summer heat and into which from the other side the tribes of the western plain also penetrated, though how far and under what conditions I did not know. To the hills therefore it was decided that I should go, though it was thought to be a bad time (in November) for meeting people there. Two letters written during and just after this journey are the last that have survived from Eritrea, so perhaps I may be forgiven one final quotation.

'We are on tour in the north of the country,' I wrote,

> with a train of camels, for the plain, and mules, for the hills. Four days ago we left all the camels behind, to take the mules up some mountains where it is impossible for a laden camel to go, and where I should have thought it impossible for a laden mule to go either, had I not seen it done! We came down again last night and this morning with empty bellies, our supplies having run out, and failed to find the camels at the rendezvous. So a couple of hours ago I was expecting to have to make a 'hunger march' today and all tomorrow, over the mountains again to where we should find some people. But Alhamdulillahi! we found our camels only an hour beyond and have eaten our fill. This is a desolate country, we have not seen a sign of human life for over twenty-four hours,

Eritrea – Hamasien, 1942–3

and the water points are very far apart. The range of hills from which we have just come down, called Hoggar Nish, is between 8000 to 9000 feet high in another world. Cold all day long I had the iciest bathe I can remember for years in a mountain pool up there. There are fields of grass and groves of juniper trees, just like Europe. It is too cold up there for the natives, who come down with their herds to take advantage of the winter rains in the Bassopiano (my present study is concerned with their nomadic movements). I bought a rug of sheep's wool made up there, dyed a rich brown with juniper wood smoke. If it isn't too heavy I'll send it home for you to keep for me – I'm afraid you won't be able to keep it in the drawing room for the smell of the woodsmoke even in the open air is pretty strong (but a grand smell though) and you may find that your best use for it is to put it at the bottom of the chest and economize on moth balls! I'm tremendously impressed with the way that these mules take their heavy loads up and down the most awkward places, and with the skill of their drivers. The usual trouble is for one of the loads to get stuck against a piece of rock, the mule doesn't realize what has happened but pulls harder than ever with the result that he would pull himself right over if he wasn't pushed back and the load levered round the projection or in extreme cases taken off altogether. And going down steep or slippery places the driver hangs on to his tail and digs his heels in – a mule will stand for anything apparently! But we shall be sending them back soon for we are now going down nearer to the coast where there is good going for camels.

The tour is going quite well from my point of view, as we were just in time to catch the inhabitants in the mountains before their seasonal migration down to the coast for pastures new and have acquired a lot of information which could never have been obtained except on the spot. Whether in times like these (what the times are incidentally I don't know, having had no news for a fortnight), this is something one ought to be doing is another question which fortunately I don't have

Colonial Postscript

to answer, having been given the job and told to get on with it.

'I am back in Nacfa now,' I wrote nine days later,

we got in the day before yesterday, since when I've been working hard to get my report written, and typed the last page of it by lamplight this evening. Usually one goes on tour and, coming back to the world again, finds that nothing has changed – stalemate in Libya, Stalingrad not fallen yet, and all that. But this time we have been without news during one of the most eventful weeks of the war [this was the advance in the Western Desert in late 1942]. We are going into Keren tomorrow, where I shall hear all about it, in the meanwhile a number of people from O.E.T.A. have already gone north, and that being so there will be no more going out on tour for a while, I can see. It was a marvellously interesting trip and I have never felt so fit. Up on the Hoggar – did I tell you? – I collected pottery fragments from a site occupied by the 'Rom' (not Romans) conquerors who were probably there between the 3rd and 6th centuries A.D. The exact identity of these people (they were probably Alexandrine Greeks) would, if properly cleared up, settle a most important point in the history of Eritrea, which is of some interest to me now. Eritrea is a melting pot of nations, the point of contact between the Abyssinians in the south, the Nile folk to the northwest, and the Arabs on the east, and before you can begin to understand its present ethnic divisions or its social structure you have to know its history for some while back.

The report written by lamplight in Nacfa together with the events it recorded and the findings in it that were never used have fallen into the limbo of the past. But before turning my back for the last time on this unique and little-known region I feel impelled to say just a few more words about its inhabitants and explain the structure of their society which is not merely nomadic but, because of the poverty of the country, one in which only the smallest of groups are able to live together. The tribes are scattered over a vast area, so that even a modest band of invaders has always been able to 'conquer' the territory, though in its turn unable to hold it for themselves if a new band, retreating under the pressure of population movements hundreds of miles away, arrives to make claims on the already insufficient resources of grass and water. I mentioned earlier how one could find traces of these successive waves of conquest in the names of the tribes but it was as clearly discoverable in the internal structure of the tribe itself, in which the 'conqueror' and the 'conquered' live side by side, to all appearances indistinguishable, though in fact distinguished unmistakably by the settled rule that while a 'conqueror' could take a wife of the 'conquered', no one of the 'conquered' could ever aspire to marry upwards; it seems that human beings wherever they may be, in British suburbs or African wildernesses, have to erect these barriers of caste or class, which the socially 'inferior' can still find tolerable if there is someone who appears to be further down the scale than themselves. One afternoon after we had been pushing and pulling our mules all day, away from the stuffy, mosquito-ridden Anseba valley up the steep mountain paths we emerged not long before sunset onto one of the high mountain pastures, or *Rora* as they are called, among the grass and trees, and found there some women winnowing the last grains of a belated harvest, tossing the wheat high into the air where the wind caught the chaff and bore it off in a great plume behind them. We stopped and spoke to them and they told us who they were, members of a sub-tribe so small and so enfeebled that even my guides had not heard of it, but they spoke with pride for all that, for their ancestors in the dim and distant past had once possessed the land, before others had come to take it from them, and others after that, so that the time must soon come when the survivors of it would be utterly extinguished and even its name no longer a memory.

The reason why so many O.E.T.A. officers had been despatched northwards was to provide a skeleton staff for the civil affairs organizations that were being set up in Cyrenaica and

Colonial Postscript

Tripolitania. Colonel Miller was among them and so might I have been if I had not been out of touch wandering about the hills. Staff now being short again ethnology had to be shelved, and I found myself posted to the Hamasien, which was the central division in the country, and the one in which Asmara was situated. Here the S.C.A.O. (Senior Civil Affairs Officer) was Lord Gerald Wellesley, later to become the Duke of Wellington – the officer who had visited me in Massawa and had caused so much surprise by insisting on paying his railway fare. That was the sort of man he was. Gerald asked two of us, the other being Freddy Nadel, an amusing character and brilliant anthropologist, to join him in setting up a mess, and together we occupied a comfortable villa set in a somewhat desiccated garden in the middle of the town, in the Via Efraim Reatto I recall, though who that worthy was I never discovered. Asmara was a highly sophisticated town, by African standards, with its main-street shops and cathedral, its hotels and nightclubs, not to mention its other less reputable places of entertainment, its Fort Baldissera where the Officer Commanding Troops lived and its Villa Vicereale where the Chief Civil Affairs Officer lived; both Brigadiers they did not get on too well together. Asmara had for some reason been treated differently from the rest of the country, since its former Governor, Barile, was still at large, as were also the Italian Commissario, Dr Lauro, and his Residente, Signor Marcucci. These latter still retained their offices in the Divisional Headquarters, where they exercised a sort of shadow administration side by side with our own. It was an odd situation, but one which I fancy Gerald rather enjoyed, since the Italians were always very correct in their behaviour and, one must admit, brought a certain polish which was often sadly lacking where the British in their army uniforms were concerned. However they were not my responsibility; Gerald looked after the town while I looked after the country, where the Italians were something of an embarrassment, though it soon became clear that even there one could not manage without them.

The Eritrean plateau was populated by people of Abyssinian

Eritrea – Hamasien, 1942–3

stock, and every yard of it – including, it was often said, the main square in Asmara itself – had at least one village or family which claimed the right to farm it, and often more than one. The population so far exceeded the cultivable resources that there was a considerable land hunger, which had been suddenly rendered acute by the return to their villages of all the demobilized soldiers and the host of minor functionaries and hangers-on who had found service under the previous administration. Many of these people found on coming home that lands previously uncultivated had been occupied by strangers, either with or without permission, it was difficult to say, and in either case native law and custom conferred certain rights on the occupants, though these could often not be accurately defined either. Other factors further complicated an already confused situation, one being the action of the Italian authorities in declaring certain land to be State property, over which concessions had been granted to Italian farmers or others. Where this had been done by due legal process we were debarred by international law from making any changes, nor would we have been particularly keen to do so, since these farms supplied food on which the garrison was very dependent. In many cases however there were difficulties in ascertaining the true facts, from the very involved Italian records. It seemed indeed that many of these cases had been allowed to drag on and on, latterly on account of the war but before that because the Italians, one suspected, had realized that any final adjudication of a dispute was bound to cause resentment and possibly unrest, whereas procrastination still kept hope alive and also helped to preserve the peace, since the contestants would not want to spoil their chance of a favourable verdict by resorting to violent action.

The Hamasien is bare and treeless with rounded hills on which the villages are clustered, the houses like the hills being low and flattened so that they follow the contour and, unless the sun is shining to catch the angle of roofs and walls, are not at first sight distinguishable from their background, or would not be but for the church which is higher than the rest, enough to break the skyline. One village glowered at another a mile or so away across a valley and this is not too imaginative a word since, in most cases, each of them had a claim or counter-claim on the land of its neighbours, which for several decades had been waiting for a settlement. On arrival at a village to hear one of these disputes one was met by the inhabitants already ranged in their contesting groups, with the women setting up a trilling of their lips which was intended as a welcome but always had to me a most sinister sound. These Abyssinians had nothing at all in common with the people of West Africa or the Upper Nile valley, being thin lipped, spare in build and with angular features. They were great mountaineers and, being born in high altitudes, made light of the hour-long climbs which a journey through the Altopiano invariably involved and which those of us brought up nearer sea level found so exhausting. Friendly they were not, though no more unfriendly than small peasant proprietors anywhere else in the world, to whom their land is their life and seems to have the first if not the only claim on their affections.

The Abyssinians are Christians, but members of a faith which has as much in common with Judaism as with Christianity. I visited many of their churches with Gerald, one of whose most endearing qualities was his frank enjoyment of sight-seeing; unlike so many Englishmen who know it all he was avid for new experience. We collected in our mess a number of paintings in the Coptic style which is crude but colourful and effective. Like our own mediaeval church frescoes, they told a story designed to arouse the emotions of an entirely illiterate congregation. One of my favourites, which has unfortunately disappeared, was a cartoon showing the fates of the saint and sinner – the latter was depicted in a tree, plucking the fruits of pleasure, while death lay in wait with his gun, the jaws of hell yawned beneath, and the two rats of night and day gnawed through the trunk which supported him. Another popular subject was St George slaying the dragon – the scene depicted on the christening plate which I bought on my first visit to Asmara – and another King Solomon and particularly his affair with the Queen of Sheba. According to one of the many traditions, she was invited by the king to a sumptuous dinner at his palace, the courses of which consisted entirely of highly spiced and salted dishes. But the poor queen was offered nothing at all to drink, and the only water to be had was from a pitcher at the king's bedside. These scenes are shown in the Abyssinian paintings as a series of incidents in a sort of strip cartoon, and they show the queen approaching the royal bed, which ecclesiastical convention places behind a pillar, so that the immediately subsequent episodes have to be imagined. In the course of time the queen gives birth to Menelik, ancestor of the Abyssinian royal house, who is recognized by King Solomon as his son. When later Menelik visited the court the king received him kindly, giving him the title of King of Sion and presenting him with retainers from the chief families in Jerusalem. It appears that the persons thus chosen viewed with little enthusiasm their transference to an unknown and pagan country and that one of their number, the son of the High Priest, stole the tables of the law and brought these away with him. Though Menelik was not himself a party to this deed he did not repudiate it and after his return home became an active propagandist of the Mosaic law. His Israelite retainers were rewarded with positions of importance up and down the country, the sons of Levi being settled in the Hamasien and the sons of Benjamin in Acchele Guzai to the south of it. We commissioned one of these Coptic church painters to make a mess portrait of Gerald, Freddy, myself and Gerald's golden retriever bitch, Gemma. The artist undertook the work but told us that no sittings were required, after all if he could manage St George and King Solomon there would be no difficulty in depicting three British army officers in uniform, except for their cap badges, with which he was unfamiliar and borrowed from us for a short while. These in the event were more recognizable than their wearers! He was even less observant about Gemma and in my version – for we had three copies made – she had changed her sex.

The most famous of the institutions of the Coptic church are its monasteries which, following the same tradition as the Greek Orthododx Church, are situated in remote places and totally

Colonial Postscript

barred to all females, even the females of animals (perhaps it was in deference to this tradition that Gemma underwent her transmutation). The best known of these in Eritrea is the one at Bizen, on a mountain peak near Asmara – where it had been built at least 500 years before Asmara was thought of. This was quite a climb, but nothing compared to the one at Zad Amba southwest of Keren. Here the chapel and the cells for the monks were perched on a ledge on a spur of the main mountain, the sole approach to which lay along a knife edge of rock with cliffs dropping away 1000 feet or more on either side. The monks here, once they had passed a certain age and lost their youthful agility, could never again return to the outer world but had to rely on all their food and other supplies being brought over by the younger monks, who unflinchingly strode across this awful chasm. Not so with me, who toiled across the ridge with legs astride it, taking a quarter of an hour to travel only 100 feet to the other side and back again, not daring to look down but conscious only of the wind, the buzzards circling overhead, and a devout hope that I was not going to provide one of them with its dinner.

Scenically the Hamasien could be most attractive, particularly in the early summer when the green of the young crops provided a vivid contrast to the rich oranges and reds of the rocky outcrops which were everywhere visible, all the details of the landscape fitting into the larger view of line upon line of hills rolling away into the distance as the eye travelled southwards towards Abyssinia. Ecologically, it was a disastrous sight, for these bare slopes, completely denuded of any permanent vegetation, offered no resistance to the sweeping rains of summer and were being eroded on a massive scale. Soil erosion is a slow process but its effects were dramatically brought home to me one day when I had gone out to the farm of an Italian concession-holder in the Pendici, or eastern slopes of the plateau. Our path led us over the bed of a dry watercourse two hundred feet across. 'You see that?' the farmer said. 'I used to be able to step across it when I first came to this country, 20 years ago.' To counter this process we started a vigorous but only partly

Eritrea – Hamasien, 1942-3

successful tree-planting campaign, using the graceful but hardy eucalyptus which would enhance the landscape besides one day providing valuable timber. However in some areas the villagers refused to cooperate, lest the planting of trees by the present occupants of disputed land might be construed on some future occasion as supporting a claim by them to permanent ownership. Gerald took a great interest in the afforestation and agricultural programmes we tried to initiate, the climax of our efforts being when we arranged in the Pendici area what was the first – and probably the last – agricultural show ever to be held in Eritrea, with prizes and certificates (written in Italian and Tigrinya) for the exhibitors, mule rides for the children, tea in a tent and the band of the Sudan Defence Force playing the Londonderry Air.

It was from the Pendici that there was the spectacular view eastwards over Massawa and the Islands described in the last chapter. On the other side going down towards the Western Plain the escarpment was almost as steep and even more inaccessible. According to the map there were two ways up it, and both of these roads were followed by the retreating Italian army when the battle for Eritrea first began. However on the southern route the mapmakers had been in advance of the roadmakers, for while one road led to the foot of the escarpment, and another led as far as its edge, the vital piece in the middle had never been completed; at this point therefore the army had had to abandon all its wheeled transport and escape on foot. That left one road, and one road only, for the invading army to obtain access to the plateau, and this lay up the Keren gorge; to anyone who has seen this it will always seem incredible that any force in the world could have taken the position by direct assault. Yet taken it was, though not without heavy cost, as a war graves cemetery at the head of the pass bears witness. Later on I made several journeys up the pass, and never ceased to wonder at the heroism of those who stormed it, but at the time about which I write I had only seen the view from the top, looking downwards. What I saw from here, mostly open country though some of it covered with scrub, its outlines quivering in

Colonial Postscript

the heat haze, was the great plain of the Southern Sahara, stretching with hardly any perceptible fall all the 3000 miles to Sokoto and beyond. The eastern extremities of this vast area, with the foothills of the mountains where I now stood, constituted the region known to the Italians as the Bassopiano Occidentale, or Western Plain, and it was the post in charge of this Division, I learned one day, that was to be my next appointment.

XI
Eritrea – Agordat, 1943–4

The Bassopiano Occidentale was Eritrea's largest division and occupied about half the country – its less attractive half, most people considered. A fair part of it was desert. The only road there dipped from Asmara to Keren, and then again down the Keren gorge to Agordat, which was the administrative headquarters of the Division. From Agordat the same road continued westwards through Barentu and Tessenei, where junior officers were stationed, and thence over the frontier to Kassala in the Sudan. There was always a fair amount of traffic between Kassala and Asmara and a lot of interesting people dropped in, sometimes for a drink and sometimes to spend the night; as they nearly always brought their own beds and servants with them this caused no domestic upheaval. Agordat was a pleasant little town, bare and dusty as I found it, now I hope with streets lined with trees, if the householders continued to carry out instructions to water the saplings and keep the goats at bay until they had established a foothold. Just down the road was the Divisional Office with a large upstairs room, well stocked with fascinating records about the early days of the Italian occupation when the Mahdi's lieutenant Osman Digma was still raiding far and wide, carrying off slaves and putting villages to the sword. Here I wrote my reports and dealt with the correspondence which accumulated while I was out of the station, heard the occasional cases and sometimes in the evening read from an Arabic version of 'Robinson Crusoe' with an ex-Sudanese schoolmaster who had settled in Agordat and was very particular about pronunciation – I had great difficulty in enunciating the 'k' sound in the hero's name to his satisfaction! The low hills in and around Agordat were brown and barren, including the small eminence where my own, the Medical Officer's and the Superintendent of Police's bungalow were situated; below and all round them there was a broad swathe of green at eye level. These were the crested tops of the dom palms which crowded the banks of the River Barca, or rather its bed, for the river itself was very rarely flowing. Of the three main water courses flowing from the Eritrean hills through the western plain only one finds its way to the Nile and so, eventually, to the sea, the other two petering out into the sand, where cotton plantations have been established to make use of their inland estuaries. Through this forest of palms (for which even the Italians had not been able to find a use, except for the making of buttons) I used to walk most mornings before breakfast, before the sun became too hot, to exercise Gemma, whom Gerald had bequeathed to me when he left Eritrea to go north to Sicily with the invading armies. Poor Gemma, she was a great companion for a while but the heat was too much for her, and my absences from Agordat for weeks at a time made it impossible to look after her. One night when left behind she got loose and picked up a piece of meat which had been baited with strychnine for the hyenas, and when I got back she was dead.

It is a pity that none of the letters home from this period have survived to help me describe the country and its inhabitants, who were as interesting and unusual as one might find anywhere in the world. The principal tribe, though it was really more a loose confederation, was the Beni Amer, one of the four main groups of the Beja people of the northeastern Sudan. Another of these groups, the Hadendoa, occupied the territory over the international border, which roughly separated the one from the other although there was much going and coming across it. These people were distinguished by mops of hair, standing six inches away from the top and side of the head, liberally anointed with butter oil and camel urine and ornamented with carved wooden combs of an intricate design. They wore a minimum of clothing but even so if one of them came into a room it was necessary to ensure that he stood in a direct line between open door and window. Their chief was the Diglal, but he had adopted a sedentary existence and grown fat, and had little standing with the tribe. He and the other elders wore turbans and the usual style of Sudanese desert robes, and they followed the Mohammedan religion, up to a point; the tribesmen were only nominally Muslim and practised none of the statutory observances of prayer, fasting and pilgrimage. The Beni Amer were almost entirely nomadic, their wealth consisting of their herds of goats and camels, whose need for pasture and water governed their movements throughout the year. Just a little grain was sown, in the sandy floor of the river bed at what was judged to be the right time, that is when the last flood water had passed over it and the ground was still damp, but of course they were often mistaken and there would be another flood which washed the seed away again.

In the confusion that followed the Italian retreat a number of tribesmen had seized the opportunity to desert, taking their rifles with them. Among them was a certain Ali Muntaz – Ali the Corporal – who became the leader of an armed band which carried out a number of raids on other tribal groups, including the Hadendoa from over the border. These raiders, or *shifta* as they are called locally, have existed since time immemorial in the broken country to the north, west and south of Abyssinia and have always been difficult to suppress, even when there is a strong government in the saddle, because of their mobility and knowledge of the country in which they operate. Usually if they surrender they do so voluntarily as a result of an amnesty, which governments find in the longer run it is cheaper to offer them than to tie up indefinitely large numbers of police and sometimes troops hunting for a quarry who has always moved on from the area in which he is being sought – sometimes 12 hours before, sometimes six or even less, when the embers of the fire on which he has cooked his meal are still warm and the dung of his camels still fresh when the police arrive in hot pursuit. Or so they said, but the free air of the desert is a wonderful magnifier of stories and I soon found that it would never be possible to separate fact from fiction without getting to know much more about all the circumstances on the spot. Besides which, it was logical to suppose that one could not properly administer a nomadic people without becoming at least semi-nomadic oneself, a line of argument which happened to coincide remarkably well with my natural inclinations. It was no great hardship to leave Agordat and the files to look after themselves and get into the saddle again.

My initiation into camel riding had taken place on an earlier trip into the mountains north of Keren, after which I wrote

> Riding a camel plays hell with your stomach when you aren't used to it. After my first long stretch of five or six hours I lay back and felt that all my intestines were painfully sorting themselves out and getting back where they belonged, which was probably very much what they were doing! The way to combat this – and fortunately I had been forewarned – is to get a long cummerbund and strap yourself round so tightly that they just have to stay put! It's a very useful thing to have in any case as at the heights at which we have been moving there is a very sudden and rapid drop in temperature when the sun goes down and it's easy to get a chill.

But this must have been just an initial experience, for my main recollection was of how accustomed I soon became to the motion and found it far more comfortable to carry on for much longer periods at a time than on horseback; on a camel one can cross one's legs in a different position over its neck every hour or so, and almost doze off at times, indeed it is said to be one of the principal hazards of camel riding over level ground, particularly at night, that one can fall asleep quite easily and then, if the camel's stride should shorten slightly for any reason, lose one's balance and fall to the ground, which is quite a long way off.

Camels are delicate creatures and do not take kindly to changes of environment; there were camels which did well in the hills and others which thrived in the Barca valley. The

Eritrea – Agordat, 1943–4

difference was mainly due to slight changes in diet, I suspect. It was difficult to get far with these questions because of the language barrier; the Beni Amer spoke Tigré which has affinities with Amharic rather than Arabic. However one could learn quite a lot from observing the skill and understanding with which they handled their valuable animals, and I shall mention some instances of these later. Travelling was a slow business for although a camel can trot quite rapidly its normal walking pace is only about three miles an hour and in open country this makes a day's journey seem interminable. One would start in the morning making for a distant hill which imperceptibly grew larger and larger until close on noon one was passing under its flanks. After that it was no longer in view but looking back in the evening it would still be in sight, low down on the horizon. The heat was pitiless, the sunlight intense; khaki shorts and shirt were bleached white and face and arms burnt khaki after some weeks of this exposure. Because of the heat we sometimes travelled at night, planning our longer trips for the second half of the month when there was a morning moon and particularly in the third quarter when its light was strongest; sometimes we would break camp soon after midnight and carry on until about eight o'clock in the morning when we lay up in whatever shade we could find of a rock or a thorn bush until mid-afternoon when we rode a further easy stage before sunset. At these halts the camels were hobbled and turned loose and then an hour before we were due to start someone would go off to find them, and always seemed to know where to look, however far they might have wandered in the meanwhile.

In retrospect and, I am sure, also at the time, the hardships of this form of travel were compensated for by some very great advantages. The chief of these was that the party was able to travel self-contained; there was no question here, as in Northern Nigeria, of dependence on a team of porters toiling away through the bush with their headloads to some predetermined destination which could no longer be changed once they had set off. Here we went where we would, sleeping in the open with our sheepskin saddle rugs laid out on the sand and a spare piece of clothing rolled up as a pillow. All our requirements for a journey of several weeks were carried in the saddle bags, a blanket, a kettle and frying pan, flour, oil and salt, while the water travelled in goatskin bottles where it kept cool by evaporation and remarkably fresh. Water, as one soon realizes in desert or semi-desert environments, is a very variable commodity and the nomads had an appreciation of it as refined as that of a Frenchman for his wine; very often we would add a further five miles to our journey or make an earlier halt because of the reputation of the quality of the local supply. Like Monsieur Besse with his coffee they were not so concerned about the appearance of the sample as with its taste, distinguishing between more 'masculine' and 'feminine' waters according to their degree of salinity. Needless to say the masculine type was the superior one!

Milk and meat were the mainstay of our rations. The former came straight from the camel, or more occasionally sheep or goat, in large gourds where an appreciable amount of foreign matter was floating. But this never did us any harm, while the milk itself was gloriously refreshing, and we warmly thanked the ladies of the encampment as we passed the bowl from hand to hand. No doubt Ali Muntaz had enjoyed similar hospitality; it seemed hardly polite to enquire. For meat there was usually a kid to be had, which was led away bleating to have its throat cut and then be skinned like a rabbit, the ribs being nicked with a dagger at the point where they joined the spine and pulled out by the teeth, one by one. It was fascinating to watch. Finally, only a few minutes later the job was finished, the skin turned right side out again and all the meat now minus the bones stowed back in the bag it formed, to be slung over the saddle ready for the evening meal. Occasionally too I got a gazelle with the British service rifle that I had tested for accuracy on a range before leaving and brought with me; the Italian rifles carried by my companions being poor stuff and their marksmanship no better. There was tremendous jubilation when the creature tumbled over in the sand and they all went racing towards it,

Eritrea – Agordat, 1943–4

daggers in hand, to slit the throat of the dying animal in the name of Allah, the Compassionate, the Merciful.

We fed apart in the evening and I suppose this was wrong but at that time I had not got to the point of abandoning knife and fork and felt that this might cause some embarrassment. However we joined up for coffee, which was the real sacrament. Its preparation was a ritual whose details I can no longer entirely recall, though I remember the earthenware pot with rounded bottom for standing in the embers, its narrow mouth stuffed with dry hair-like grass to form a percolator, which was thrice brought to the boil and thrice removed to cool before the contents, spiced with ginger, were poured into tiny cups. These, held between thumb and forefinger, were lifted with a characteristic tilt of the fingers to the mouth, and the heavily sugared mixture sipped with resounding satisfaction.

The Beni Amer way of life had changed little since the days of the Pharaohs and the books of Genesis and Exodus could still serve as a manual for modern administration. I was often reminded of the conversation between Abraham and Lot: 'let there be no strife, I pray thee,' says Abraham,

> between me and thee, and between my herdsmen and thy herdsmen; for we be brothers. Is not the whole land before thee? Separate thyself, I pray thee, from me; if thou wilt take the left hand, then I will go to the right; or if thou depart to the right hand, then I will go to the left. (Genesis 13)

Just like two Beni Amer heads of families working out their grazing programme. In this community one offence was repaid by another, according to the old Mosaic rule of retaliation. There was a system of compounding the offence by a suitable fine which the Italians had tried to popularize but the people did not think much of it and to us the scale of charges seemed altogether too high. Ken Trevaskis told me of his remonstrating with a local chief about the compensation payable for abducting a virgin, a not uncommon episode in tribal warfare, which ran to a colossal number of camels.

Colonial Postscript

'How can you justify such a penalty?' he demanded.

'Ah,' said the greybeard, with a twinkle in his eye, 'but you see our virgins are worth it.'

All the while the raids continued, with the Beni Amer stealing camels, goats and, when they could get them, virgins from the Hadendoa, and the Hadendoa raiding back, though not with the same vigour since they had not inherited any Italian army rifles. Occasionally someone on one side or the other got killed. It was a serious matter, taking place across an international boundary, and the Sudanese authorities looked askance at us for failing to control our tribesmen, though they understood the problem well enough to appreciate our difficulties. We had all run out of ideas about what to do next, and it occurred to me that it might be worthwhile to consult a man reputed by the Beni Amer to be a saint, who lived an isolated life in a remote valley. One day, when touring in the area, I went to visit him, feeling slightly self-conscious about doing so, like one of those who had gone out to call on John the Baptist, and wondering quite how I would reply if asked the question 'What went you out into the wilderness to see?'. But the saint was cagey or, if he delivered himself of any memorable remarks, they were lost in the translation. I was not the only one concerned, as the tribal leaders were worried too; their young men had got out of hand and their own authority was being undermined. So it was decided to hold a conference to try to establish the facts and organize a settlement. The meeting was fixed for Christmas, at Kassala in the Sudan, to which I now paid my first visit, in the company of the Diglal and other tribal leaders.

Kassala was a dream of delight. Christmas is a dried up time of year in Africa south of the Sahara but here the roads were flanked by trees as in an English suburb and the Residency garden boasted a superb lawn, product of goodness knows how much patience and irrigation, surrounded by shady trees and the continuous song of birds. Here was the same handful of British officers as in a Northern Nigerian provincial headquarters, but doing business in Arabic instead of Hausa, and administering even vaster areas. Kassala Province alone was 700 miles from end to end, and it was by no means the largest. While I relaxed in the congenial atmosphere the leaders of the two tribes got down to work, each side drawing up a debit list of offences agreed to have been committed by its own tribesmen against the other and a credit list of the flocks and herds alleged to have been stolen and the individuals killed, wounded, raped or removed. The second lists were so wildly exaggerated and the first so considerably understated that for a couple of days the talks made no progress. It was only on the third day that the negotiators, tiring of the proceedings and wanting to return home, began to strike out the claims not sufficiently supported by evidence and to allow those that were. On the fourth day a grand balance sheet was struck of all the claims and counter-claims. This as foreseen was much in favour of the Hadendoa, to whom the Beni Amer had to accept an undertaking to pay, over the next 12 months, a considerable sum in compensation. Finally the chiefs and their followers adjourned to the tomb of the Said el Mirghani, where they swore to accept the pact and to live in amity in future.

Soon after we had returned home and were working out how the liability should be fairly divided between the different sections of the tribe – a liability which would involve the rounding up and compulsory sale of livestock, since there was no other way of meeting it – the young men who cared not at all about what their elders had agreed to were once again on the warpath. It was a depressing outlook because at best the whole dispute could only be brought to an end by collective punishments which would impoverish the entire tribe, while at worst there could be a continuing pattern of raids and counter-raids growing in intensity and endangering the peace not only of the Beni Amer but of their neighbours as well.

Asmara was naturally concerned about the situation, the blame for which fell mainly on the police, though in fact because of their deficiencies in training and equipment the problem had become too big for them. At this stage therefore it was decided to hold an Army exercise down in the Bassopiano which would at least create an impression that something was being done. So for the next month or so the troop carriers of the Sudan Defence Force milled about the more accessible parts of the Western Plain or got stuck trying to cross the deep sand of its wadis, lagering up in encampments at night, from which their commander wirelessed to me his report on the day's events, in code of course, the message invariably reaching me at one o'clock in the morning. It was a splendid exercise for the troops even if totally irrelevant to the actual situation, for no sooner had they returned to base than the tribal forays began once more across the border. On the other hand the collective penalties imposed on the Beni Amer may have caused pressure to be brought on Ali Muntaz who, when an amnesty was offered – not in my time but in that of my successor – surrendered himself to the authorities. Perhaps we did after all succeed in making life more uncomfortable for him than we realized. Another result was the decision to station a detachment of the Sudan Defence Force camel corps in Agordat, which involved a certain amount of new construction at the other end of the town, the funds for which passed through my office; this was the first and only occasion in my life that I have had any repsonsibility, however indirect, for building a brothel!

There is a postscript to be added. Because of their preoccupation with this family feud with the Hadendoa, the Beni Amer failed until it was too late to realize what alternatives were open to them when the final settlement of the Italian colonies fell due to be made after the war. Geographically the Western Plain of Eritrea formed part of the Sudan; its people were of the same race, spoke the same language and followed the same way of life as their cousins over the border. They had nothing in common with the Amharic people of the Abyssinian plateau, and had received nothing from them in the course of history except neglect and oppression. Here there would have been a chance, in one small corner of the continent, to redraw the map so that the political boundaries would follow the proper ethnic and economic divisions instead of the arbitrary lines which had been imposed by the European powers during the 19th-century scramble for Africa. But nothing came of the opportunity and in

Eritrea – Agordat, 1943–4

the end Abyssinia got the whole country of Eritrea, both plain and plateau, to have and to hold, but certainly not to love and to cherish. And so it remained until the next historical convulsion – which was to occur sooner than anyone expected. At the time it looked as though the present century would have no more noticeable effect on the lives and customs of the inhabitants of this region than the twenty or more which had preceded it.

Many years after leaving the country I presented the Imperial War Museum in London with my set of the 'handkerchief' maps of the northern part of Eritrea, of a scale approximately four miles to the inch, which had been compiled and 'zincographed' at the Survey Office, Khartoum, in 1940, in preparation for the allied offensive. These maps were printed on linen, so that they could be stuffed into a saddle bag or put away in a trouser pocket. Like Swift's geographers, who

> ... o'er uninhabitable downs
> Place elephants, for want of towns

the Sudan surveyors also gave way, if not to imagination, to something not far removed from it. The principal features of the terrain are quite often supplemented by verbal descriptions; thus on Sheet 55D, 'Khor Langeb is a broad wadi fringed with tamarisk and Dom palms and running between fairly high hills. Wild asses frequent it'. (What echoes of the *Rubaiyat*!) Some of these notes about what are or are not alleged to be features to be seen en route are particularly tempting to the traveller, such as one on Sheet 46M which comments, 'Khor Onal rises from a valley in the middle of Jebel Tiaiye, to which there is only access on foot, and escapes S.E. into Eritrea through a narrow precipitous gorge impassable to animals. This valley used to be a great robber stronghold.' And elsewhere, 'Round Jebel Moman are curious ruins of stone tombs with one very small entrance. Building very neat dry packing – sometimes two, sometimes three tiers but the top is always circular and the bottom square'. The robber stronghold I did not and now alas shall never see, but I inspected many of the tombs, both on my previous trips to the northern hills and now again in the course of another journey in the same direction, this time following the course of the Anseba where it wound through the hills to join the Barca close to where it crossed the frontier into the Sudan.

Rom, said the Beni Amer when they saw the tombs, as they might have said 'bush' or 'star' or 'mountain', or anything else that was part of nature rather than the work of men's hands. They were too occupied with the hard business of living to have much curiosity for these monuments of a past, which appeared totally unconnected with their own lives. In fact they did not often pass this way themselves. It was the object of my third and last visit to the northern mountains, but this time to the western side of them, to see just what the population consisted of, for the police maintained no post in the area, and sent no patrols, so no reports of it ever came out and it seemed to me (especially on the evidence of the map) to be a possible hide-out to which fugitives might betake themselves if the more open country to the south was made too hot for them. But we found it almost totally deserted, and travelled for days seeing neither man nor beast, nor signs that any had been there. It was an empty rugged wilderness, devoid of any vegetation except for a few thorn bushes here and there in a sheltered corner. Water holes were few and far between. By day dust storms blew continuously and we travelled as much as we could by night, the camels padding silently over the sandy floor of the valleys on which the steep cliffs cast inky shadows in the moonlight. 'Woe to the land shadowing with wings which is beyond the rivers of Ethiopia,' wrote Isaiah, perhaps with the valley of the lower Barca in mind. 'The burden of the desert of the sea. As whirlwinds in the south pass through; so it cometh from the desert, from a terrible land.'

Turning south once more we came again to the main grazing grounds of the Beni Amer in the centre of the province and spent some days among them seeking information about their numbers and their movements. One day when I was travelling ahead of the main party alone except for a single companion my camel went lame; this had never happened to me before and fortu-

Eritrea – Agordat, 1943–4

nately this time the incident occurred not more than a few miles from the encampment of a group which had the reputation of being extremely skilled in the care of these animals. How well justified this was I soon discovered. One of the tribesmen came out of his tent, glanced at the camel and, without even requiring to see it walk, pierced a vein in its leg with the point of his dagger and, after allowing the puncture to bleed freely for some minutes, bound it again with a piece of bark stripped from the nearest thorn tree. Half an hour later I was riding the camel again, all trace of the limp having vanished. Bloodletting and branding are the main tools of primitive medicine and the Beni Amer practised both, on their animals and on themselves. The camels had to be securely bound before the operation could be performed, their legs trussed beneath them, their head strapped to their side, but still they rolled around in agony when the hot iron was applied. Brand marks were a frequent sight on the chests of men and women too; the purpose appeared to be to remove one source of pain by creating another.

Towards the end of May 1944 three friends held a reunion in an obscure valley off the Upper Barca, where our three Divisions met; these were Ken Trevaskis from Keren, Jack Crawford from Adi Ugri in the Serae and myself from the Bassopiano Occidentale. The official reason for our meeting was to look jointly into a dispute which involved trespass by the nomad herdsmen (my Beni Amer of course!) onto the cultivations of the settled farmers, belonging to Ken and Jack, an age-old dispute for which I very much doubt that we were able or even tried very hard to find a solution. For the real reason was to celebrate my 30th birthday, which we did to such good effect that my companions decided to sleep through the afternoon and return in the evening. But for some reason I wanted to hurry on by the direct route to Asmara, and all through the heat of the day with the sun on my back toiled up the escarpment, looking back whenever I paused at the gradually extending view over the grey-green plain of Africa and the blue of its far horizon. My thoughts returned to a similar ascent on the mountains of Cumbria – could it really be only ten years ago that I had been plodding up the long slopes of Scafell pondering on what to do when my university days would soon be over? And I remember as the day declined, the air grew cool and I emerged at last on the level plateau, my feeling of thankfulness that these ten years had been so very, very good.

XII
Singapore, 1945–6

I had gone off on home leave in the summer of 1944 hoping to return to Eritrea with my wife, who had been left behind in England after just a few weeks of marriage, and the two and a half-year-old daughter whom up to now I had not seen. A number of British wives, and families too, had made their way there, somehow circumventing the official ban. After so long spent in the plains I felt I could reckon on being posted to the Altopiano, where the climate was as good as any to be found in Africa. But I found the War Office had no intention, yet, of providing passages for families. Instead, I met Major General Hone, who had been with us in the Middle East, and who was now engaged in building up a staff of officers for a future British Military Administration of Malaya. He invited me to join him. Malaya was at that time in the hands of the Japanese who would, it was thought, strongly resist any attempt to dislodge them. No one outside a small circle knew about the atomic bomb, and even those who did could not have guessed the effect it would have on the military and political situation. It looked as though we were in for a long wait, which would give me time to get to know my family again. Accordingly I accepted his invitation and, when my leave expired, took on the job of instructing others in the principles and procedures of military administration, with which everyone – except myself – assumed that I must be familiar.

My introduction to Malaya and its civil service took place at Southlands, a women's college on Wimbledon Common which had been requisitioned by the Army and was being used as a

Colonial Postscript

Civil Affairs staff training centre. Most of the instructors had served in one or other of the Occupied Enemy Territory administrations and had a practical experience of how military government worked; now we had to teach the theory. Most of the pupils were former officers of the Malayan Public Works services, a Department which had ordered its staff out of the country in the last days before the capitulation, in order that their technical skills might be put to use in other territories. Their experience of African and other colonies seemed to have been mainly unhappy ones and they were all looking forward to returning to a familiar and, one gathered, more enlightened environment. Among the subjects they had to be taught was how to write reports, Army-style. At the end of the lecture one of them was asked how he would set about this. 'I would get the chief clerk to look up last year's,' he replied. But would there be any last year's report, or a chief clerk to find it? The fact of the matter was that almost nothing was known about what had been going on in Malaya during the years that had passed since the fall of Singapore in February 1942. It could be assumed that stocks of food must be very low and that little had been done in the way of repairs or renewals. But no detailed information had come out of the country, nor could anyone guess what action the Japanese commanders would take if they decided to defend it. It took everyone by surprise that the surrender when it came was a peaceful one.

By bad luck I arrived too late to see it. My troop carrier broke down in the Indian Ocean and I had a frustrating wait of a fortnight in Ceylon – though if one had to wait in idleness anywhere, Peradeniya gardens at Kandy, where 'SACSEA' (Supreme Allied Commander, South East Asia, to the initiated!) had his headquarters, was not a bad place to do it. Only one incident took place there which is worth recording. This was when a party of officers, including myself, went out into the country to inspect a possible site for a transit camp. All of us trudged over the area except one, who remained in the car. He explained that in private life he was a civil servant in the Treasury, and that it was his practice never to look at things on

Singapore, 1945–6

the ground, but only to read the case that had been put up about them in the file, as otherwise he might get his judgments wrong! Eventually, when other transport had been found, I continued the journey to Singapore, arriving there in the first week of October 1945. I was wrong in saying that none of my letters remain from this period; my mother evidently kept a few of the earlier ones, from which I will now quote.

> This is the address, and the photograph shows where it is situated – the long building with the pillars in front of it overlooking the *padang* where football matches are played and demonstrations (all of them loyal so far!) are staged. The building next door with the dome is the Supreme Court, or was; I'm not sure whether it still is or even if there is such a thing as a Supreme Court at the moment. I came ashore on the afternoon of the 5th and reported my arrival to the appropriate authorities who sent me to Singapore Division where I found to my surprise that the job which I had been casually promised months ago in London was still open – with the appropriate rank too. I began work the next day which for some time will consist of getting the hang of things in the enormously complex structure which B.M.A. [British Military Adminstration] has already become, within a few weeks of having begun to operate in the country. So different from the early days of O.E.T.A. Eritrea, which was almost the first military government ever, and started from scratch, practically contemporaneously with the entry of the troops, whereas B.M.A. Malaya has been planned and organized for the past two years . . . As, for the first time in my life, I am office-bound, seeing the world at second hand in the pages of files, I'm afraid that my impressions will be superficial. Singapore is little battle-scarred but very dowdy; nothing has had a lick of paint for years (except the fire station) and the Japs – or Nips as they are universally called – were a dirty crowd of people, not a bit like what they are reputed to be in their own land. It is almost completely a Chinese city; there are few Malays about at all. I formed a favourable impression

Colonial Postscript

of the Chinaman from the moment I landed and chartered a Chinese 'driven' bicycle rickshaw to take me and my kit along (these cycle taxis are a product of the war here, as in Paris). The Chinese are uncommonly virile and energetic, most unlike the Africans! The size of Singapore is vast, it is as large as a fair size city in England.

This letter brings back first impressions I could easily have forgotten. The most immediate was the contrast between the style and scale of Singapore, compared with any African colonial towns I had visited. The municpal building (the one with the pillars, prestigious but quite non-functional) housed the military administration during its first few months, while the more homely (though architecturally no less bizarre) Colonial Secretariat building was, like Government House itself, still occupied by the Army. Within days of settling down to work there began the long drawn out paper battle between the Civil Affairs branch who argued that they could not do their job to satisfy the population unless schools, hospitals, business premises and civilian accommodation were released, and the Army, who replied that they were doing their best, that demobilization was proceeding as fast as ships could be found to take away men and stores, but anyway was it so certain that the civil administration was firmly enough established to be able to take over? Unexpected things were happening in the neighbouring territories of French Indo-China and the Dutch East Indies, and there might be surprises to come in Malaya too.

'I went to a service in St Andrew's cathedral,' the next letter records. This was a large building (said to be the only cathedral built by a Public Works Department; it possessed some astonishingly beautiful stained glass) standing on the other side of the Municipal Offices,

> the church was packed with a cosmopolitan gathering of men and women of the three services, British, Indian and Malay, and with Eurasian, Malay, Chinese and Indian civilians. I had a Chinese lady in front of me, neatly and attractively dressed,

Singapore, 1945-6

with two little Chinese girls. It was a full choral eucharist, with mostly the same antiphons as they have at Chewton Mendip – a good choir, as mixed as the congregation, and a Chinese lady organist. Although it was efficiently organized, the congregation was so large that the service took an hour and a quarter to get through ... I believe that the services in the cathedral were never discontinued (during the Japanese occupation), as a Ceylonese priest was left at liberty – though every single prayer with a reference to the Royal family had been pasted over in the book I was using.

No special summons had been needed to bring this great number of people to the cathedral this Sunday, but a feeling of thankfulness to be alive which all the races could share, however different the views they held about the future of the country which had just been liberated, from near-starvation as well as from the Japanese. Some of these differences were obvious. Looking through the open doors of the cathedral at the grass and trees of the *padang*, and the ships beyond lying at anchor in the bay, one could just see on the water front the stub of a memorial to the Indian National Army – made up of Indian troops who had defected to the enemy – which the Royal Engineers, on landing in Singapore, had considered it their first duty to blow up, before proceeding to their other business. But a month or two later, the security forces in the city were all agog because Lord Mountbatten, the 'Supremo', had invited Pandit Nehru, the leader of Indian nationalism, to visit Singapore and stay with him – a tactless and probably embarrassing gesture, many of the senior officers thought. The Indian population, which formed only a small part of the island's inhabitants but accounted for more than half of the large labour force employed by the Services, the Military Administration and the Municipality, was already showing an inconvenient degree of political self-consciousness, and it was feared that a visit from their leader could only make matters worse. But Nehru behaved with the utmost discretion. In duty bound to pay a visit to the site of the I.N.A. memorial, he did so at 6.30 a.m., when there were few about to see him. Addressing an Indian audience which had crammed the stadium to hear him, he told them plainly that there should be no thoughts of dual nationality in their calculations; their future in Malaya was to be found in supporting local political organizations, not in being supported by Indian ones. All this could not have been more helpful. Later in the day he was entertained to dinner by the Chinese Chamber of Commerce, a test of stamina which only those who have experienced such hospitality can properly evaluate, and late, very late in the evening came to address a press conference in the Adelphi hotel. The assembly of newsmen who had been waiting some hours for his arrival, wilting in the heat of the airless room, sprang to life as he entered and, without a pause to acclimatize himself to his audience, launched into an account of his policy, the vision of India as he saw it, a magnificent off-the-cuff oration, with past, present and future rolled up into one. Questions followed, including an awkward one which Nehru neatly parried, raising a sympathetic laugh against the aggressive Anglo-Indian journalist who had asked it. At 12.30 a.m. most men would have been content to leave it at that. 'But this is not what you meant, is it?' asked Nehru, when the laughter had subsided, and he proceeded first to rephrase the question in an even more difficult form, and then to answer it in detail. Such intellectual honesty is rare.

By now the period of military government was drawing to an end. Wives began to appear (greatly complicating the accommodation problem by doing so!) and officers of the pre-war Malayan Civil Service started to return from post-internment leave. Except for the Public Works Department, who had been given special dispensation, most of the civil servants had felt it their duty to remain at their posts as the Japanese advanced. Only after the surrender did a few manage to get away – and were never quite forgiven by their imprisoned colleagues for doing so. The argument was that a service which identified itself at all other times with the country and its people could not, when disaster struck, seek for itself a different fate from the rest of the population. It was an honourable, but disappointing,

Singapore, 1945–6

logic. For the invaders, on their side, discriminated very sharply between the expatriate Europeans, who were imprisoned or interned at a barely tolerable level of subsistence, and the native Malays, Chinese and Indians, who were left to fend for themselves, which meant in many cases to die of malnutrition. And when at last the liberating forces arrived, the internees and prisoners were not allowed to join the population at liberty, but sent home on recuperation leave, so that they played no part in the first few months of reorganization.

Their return was awaited with some apprehension by the caretaking force which had been administering civil affairs in their absence. Those of us who had been imported from African and other territories to help fill the gap wondered what account we would be held to give of our stewardship when the professionals arrived to take over! This concern was unnecessary for, in Singapore at any rate, conditions were as strange to them as to us; the war had swept away many of the former landmarks and it was even an advantage sometimes not to know they had been there. If times had been normal the differences resulting from our separate training and approach to problems might have been more apparent. The manner of life, the historical background, the place in the world of Singapore, constantly underlined these differences, the chief of which was the much greater sophistication of government business, which presented the officials day by day with problems of a complexity that would rarely be met with in other colonial territories. The M.C.S. in Singapore had to take decisions which would be studied by the keenest minds in London and evaded by the keenest wits in Asia, a situation which allowed little margin for error. Playing tennis with this sort of opponent one naturally improved one's own game. The drawback of working on this exalted plane was that one learnt nothing at first hand about what went on outside. There seemed to be no points of contact between the administrator at his desk and the crowds who filled the streets and the noisome river which flowed past the Secretariat with noise, colour and confusion. We were completely alien to one another. 'The occupation taught . . . the true

Colonial Postscript

value of freedom and of free institutions,' sententiously observed the colony's annual report. But how did its writer – who was myself – know this? To find out what people were thinking we had to turn up the police intelligence reports, but in Africa we would have expected to write them ourselves.

In Africa however, the people did not speak Chinese. In Singapore four-fifths of the population (a much higher proportion than elsewhere in Malaya) spoke one of its three or four principal dialects and nothing else. Pre-war, the Government's way of dealing with this situation had been to select a few of each year's M.C.S. cadets – it appears in a fairly arbitrary manner – and pack them off to mainland China, where they spent the next year or two learning Chinese and absorbing the Chinese way of life. From this they emerged as marked men – whether for better or worse was naturally a matter of opinion, though it would be fair to observe that the world of learning, at any rate, would have been the poorer without their scholarship. Back in Malaya, they were posted to a separate Chinese Secretariat, which of course encouraged them to identify themselves more closely with this part of the population and caused the Japanese, who had been at war with China for some years before the invasion of Malaya, to regard them with the gravest suspicion. Many were beaten up, or tortured, besides suffering the other indignities which the conquerors reserved for the expatriate population in their so-called 'co-prosperity sphere'.

There was no chance at all of a Chinese Nehru appearing on the scene to adjure his compatriots to confine Chinese politics to China. The Chinese believed that the war in the Far East had been fought and won by them. They knew nothing about the atom bomb or the American Pacific Fleet and, so far as Mountbatten's forces were concerned, they regarded them as merely stepping into a vacuum caused by the Japanese departure, and not as in any way contributing to it. To the politically-minded among them the liberation of Singapore in the late summer of 1945 was no more than an exchange of one set of imperialist masters for another, the British being preferred only because, being non-Asian and a lot less ruthless, it was thought

Singapore, 1945-6

to be easier to get rid of them. During the period of the occupation a guerilla force of Chinese had been in existence in Malaya and in the last few months it had become active; now came the problem, identical in many ways with that encountered in post-war Europe, of persuading its leaders that their task was done, and the sword should be converted into the ploughshare, or its Far Eastern equivalent. This operation was only partially successful and the leaders went to ground, to appear later as the 'bandits' or rebel organizations who were to keep a large British force pinned down in the country from 1949 onwards. At this distance of time one can see that this was no reflection on the British administration, but a confrontation which had to take place between communism and democracy and which could have ended in a different way than it did.

In Singapore the test came sooner than on the mainland, at a time when the newly recruited police force was underpowered and undermanned, although the military strength in the island was still considerable, and available to back it. During the early months of 1946 one strike followed another, aggravated by shortage of food and the high cost of living, though they were all political rather than economic in their origins. It seemed that a challenge of some kind was in prospect, and certain that if it occurred it would be met with firmness, for the officer in charge of the civil affairs branch, Brigadier McKerron, was not one who hesitated to make up his mind. So, when a general strike was called, and bands of rioters appeared in the streets, they found all the forces of law and order mobilized to meet them. One of these bands coming in from the east side of the city met the police head on at a junction with the Bras Basah road, where two of us from the Secretariat witnessed the clash from the balcony of a school building. It was fortunate that we were there because the sound of the firing brought to the scene a considerable number of journalists who had been attending a press briefing at the Supremo's headquarters in the Cathay building just round the corner. When they arrived it was mostly over, except for a few bodies lying about on the pavement. The next morning the city was back at work, and the newspapers full of accounts of British brutality, but the episode may have been more critical than any of us supposed. For, while this was not the last time that a communist minority unsuccessfully challenged the regime, it was the first time that the people of Singapore showed unmistakably that they had no wish to follow them. The military administration had only a few weeks left to run, but the Colonial Government which was to succeed it also had only a few years, during which time the 'free institutions' of democracy had to be established, hopefully on a permanent footing. This important task could now be taken in hand without risk of interruption.

XIII
Singapore continued, 1946–8

The changeover from a military to a civil administration took place in April 1946 without formality, apart from the swearing-in of Brigadier McKerron as Acting Governor and his removal from our office to the solitary splendours of Government House. For the rest of us, who came into the office wearing our badges of rank one day, and without them the next, the same problems arose and the same files were dealing with them. Since my arrival in Singapore some six months earlier I had – after some difficulty in finding anyone to teach me – been trying to learn Malay. This was partly so as not to appear wanting in the eyes of the old hands of the M.C.S. and partly in preparation for the posting to some remote district office which past experience had led me to expect. This posting would almost certainly have to be on the mainland, as there were only two 'out stations' under Singapore's jurisdiction. One of these was Christmas Island, which I knew about from boyhood days as being a lonely outpost whose letters were delivered by being dropped overboard in a barrel by the mailships en route for Australia. (What the islanders did with any letters they might wish to have collected was not revealed.) Here the inhabitants were all Chinese, who worked the phosphate deposits, and so the District Officer had to be a Chinese-speaking cadet. The other, where the inhabitants spoke Malay, was the Cocos-Keeling group of islands, tiny specks of land half way between Ceylon and Australia, and I might have gone for a spell there, if Pat had not cabled at that point to say she had secured passages for herself and the children, now two in

Colonial Postscript

number; it was clear that she would expect me to be in Singapore to meet them all, not a thousand miles away in the Indian Ocean.

So I stayed on in my job in the Secretariat, where the work was never-ending, and the main reason for the existence of weekends seemed to be to enable one to catch up with the backlog left over from weekdays. I have been trying to recall some of the problems we had to deal with. More of these later, but first a few words about how government itself was organized. There can surely never have been a place with such a top hamper of bureaucracy as Singapore just after the war. Our own particular bit of it, the Colonial Secretariat, was the top of a pyramid with hardly any base, since all local government business was handled by the Municipality, which also provided services for the parts of the island lying outside the municipal boundaries. Economic affairs were not our concern, being handled by a separate Economic Secretariat in a nearby building, and establishment matters were dealt with by a department situated in Kuala Lumpur, since there was one civil service for both the Federation and ourselves. External affairs, including defence, were the province of the Governor-General, who tactfully resided over the causeway at Johore Bahru, though his office too was in Singapore. Our own Governor, who arrived rather late to take up his appointment, since he was one of those who had been interned by the Japanese, maintained (as was the normal practice) his own separate office in Government House. There, boxes containing files requiring his attention were sent, minuted in blue or black ink to 'Y.E.' – 'Your Excellency' – by the Secretariat, to be returned minuted in red ink, a colour reserved for 'H.E.' – 'His Excellency' – as he was referred to, in the third person. (The only other privileged colour was green, which was reserved for the auditors.) When the Governor arrived in the Colony, there was a military band to play the opening bars of the national anthem, with a guard of honour for him to inspect, the same again when he was sworn in, when he left the colony, when the Colonial Secretary was sworn in as Acting Governor in his place. All this was an aspect of colonial administration which was quite new to me and I found it slightly ridiculous, but the principal actors took it all very seriously.

There was also a high degree of formality in the communications between the Governor and the Secretary of State at home, with numbered despatches couched in elegant phrases, drafted and redrafted to express the most precise nuances of opinion. We at the lower levels of the Secretariat used to have fun including in our first drafts relatively rare words which would be likely to cause our seniors to look them up in their dictionaries, and would scan the final version with interest to see if they had survived all the various revisions. Every despatch ended with the time-honoured phrase 'I have the honour to be' (one line), 'Sir,' (next line), 'your obedient servant' (third line), and then the signature. One heaved a sigh of relief after it had gone, knowing that a couple of weeks, at least, must pass before a reply could be expected. That, of course, was the drawback; the traditional method of communicating took far too long. Fairly soon despatches were superseded by 'savingrams' (hideous word), at first only on matters which were not, or were supposed not to be of sufficient weight to involve the Secretary of State, but before long for all manner of business. The day of the carefully thought-out phrase had gone, and with it disappeared much of the careful thinking. Another far-reaching change was brought about by the introduction of photocopying. I remember the exact moment when this happened. After the Colonial Secretary's office had been going for a few weeks, but before the establishment of the Economic Secretariat, there arrived one day from London an enormous bundle of correspondence relating to a cargo of rubber which had been lost or damaged in the bombardment of Singapore harbour by the Japanese four years previously. Evidently the Colonial Office had played along with the claim for a year or two, waiting to see what would happen, and had then put it on one side for a future Singapore government to deal with. One could hardly complain about that, but one's sense of propriety was outraged by the fact that instead of a précis being made, which would have been the expected thing in the past, the whole correspon-

Colonial Postscript

dence had been run through a machine so that the labour of unravelling it could be transferred from Whitehall to Singapore. I spent days on the job, which was not merely tedious but hard on the eyes, since these early photocopies were negatives, white typing on a black background.

The formalities of government were mirrored in the non-governmental, business sector, where likewise much attention was given to hierarchy and questions of precedence. Pre-war Singapore had been described, not unfairly it seems, as a 'qualified plutocracy', largely managed by and in the interests of the 'tycoons'. This word, of Japanese origin, was a title applied formerly to a hereditary commander-in-chief, which approximates to how the heads of the big business houses regarded themselves. My uncle by marriage, chairman of Paterson & Simons, East India merchants had been one of them – I knew the style in which he lived in England and now passed his palatial mansion in Singapore on my daily journeys to the office. These firms carried enormous prestige, and a rigid division existed between the seniors, who were allowed to sign 'per pro' for the company, and could put up for membership of the Singapore club, and the rest. It was like being awarded one's house colours at school. Post-war the system was not so strict, but protocol was, as I soon discovered, a serious matter. It had cropped up in one of the letters written within a few months of my arrival.

> Questions of precedence involving a Governor General, two Governors, H.M. Special Commissioner and a Supreme Allied Commander are bad enough, but there is all the consular staff to be reckoned with – Consuls General, Consuls, Acting Consuls, Vice Consuls, Counsellors in charge, not to mention various Trade Commissioners and Representatives of the Governments of India and Ceylon. Which comes first, an Acting Consul General or a Roman Catholic Archbishop?

These dignitaries, or more particularly their wives, were ready to pounce if one got it wrong, as I had done with the Attorney General, whose wife complained of not being given a sufficiently

Singapore continued, 1946-8

prominent seat among the spectators at the first formal session of the newly-appointed Legislative Council. A major test came with the arrangements for the King's birthday celebrations. Behind the saluting base was a small stand, with sufficient seats for the members of the Legislative and Executive Councils, and the very senior service commanders. All other invited guests were in two long stands, on either side of the base, green tickets giving admission to the one on the right, red to the one on the left. The day after the parade the telephone never stopped, the red ticket holders wanting to know why they had not been put in the green stand, and vice versa. They grudgingly accepted the explanation, that this depended on whether their names began with A to K, or L to Z, the alphabet providing the one basis for setting people in order with which, I have found, they do not quarrel.

Three-quarters of the population of Singapore were Chinese. Among them were families which had lived there for generations, and retained customs which had died out in their own country. A little way from our house in Ridley Park there was a kerbside seller, a woman of no great age, who had bound feet which made it impossible for her to do more than hobble, and I once even saw a male Chinese with a pigtail which, when he removed his skull cap, fell down to his waist. But most were comparatively recent immigrants, who had flooded across the sea from their own overcrowded and, at that time, politically disturbed country to make a new life and, in some cases, a fortune. Coming mainly from the lower strata of society they were no more to be regarded as representative of their national culture than, say, the Irish communities of Liverpool or Glasgow. Their energy and initiative compelled admiration, while their clannishness and traditional hostility towards foreigners – who, if not Chinese, must be inferior – repelled it. However this apparent rudeness of their behaviour may have been due to the difficulties of communication which I have mentioned earlier, and those who had seen their conduct under the Japanese occupation praised them for their courage and loyalty. Working in the Secretariat I had few contacts with them, but one in particular lingers in my memory. This was when Pat and I went to an exhibition laid on by the Chinese Chamber of Commerce, where local artists displayed their work, and we bought a lovely ink and brush drawing for, I think about 200 Straits dollars, or £24, quite a lot of money in those days, particularly as it was the only picture in the exhibition which found a buyer. The artist who came to bring it to me the next day, when the exhibition had closed, was so thrilled with the recognition of his talents that of his own accord he presented me with a second picture, in the same style and equally delightful. It was the sort of spontaneous gesture that one never forgets. We can only admire these works of art in what the Chinese would consider an ignorant fashion. To them the poem beside the picture illustrates the picture as much as the picture illustrates the poem, the calligraphy of which is equally important with what it says. This particular picture showed three fish rising to the surface of a pool where a trailing branch of bamboo, disturbed by the wind, has created a slight ripple. While the poem, it was explained to us, alludes to an exiled poet of former times who feels the breeze and is reminded by it of his distant homeland and of the fish which frequented its rivers. Few Westerners, even if they could read and translate the text, would fathom this meaning and, I would imagine, not many Chinese either.

Pat herself was an artist, at that time specializing in portraiture, for which her new life in Singapore offered boundless possibilities. Her first models were our own household staff, Malay-speaking Javanese, always very content to take time off their work to sit for her. The relationship between artist and model is a close one, and on coming home in the evenings I would be amazed to find how, with only a few dozen words of Malay at her disposal, she had been able to elicit their past histories and gain deep insights into their thoughts and patterns of behaviour. One portrait led to another, a Boianese driver from the office presented himself at the weekend, or a friend from the Social Welfare Department, who had commissioned a portrait of his Chinese wife, sent along his Sikh storekeeper for a couple of sittings. Sometimes an opportunity had to be

Singapore continued, 1946–8

snatched at short notice, as when a Public Works Department contractor doing a job on the house next door left his labourers unoccupied one morning. These were Cantonese women, wearing their traditional blue tunics surmounted by a folded red headdress reminiscent of a Holbein painting, one of whom was persuaded to sit just long enough for her portrait to be drawn in pastel and charcoal. Almost all of these portraits were subsequently sold but, before dispersal, some of them were, with the approval of my bosses in the Secretariat and with the wholehearted co-operation of the Government printer, for whom it was a job quite out of the usual run, used to illustrate the wide diversity of the colony's population in the Singapore annual reports for 1946 and 1947. This break with past tradition was well received by the local press and gratefully acknowledged by H.E. himself, no less, who wrote to the artist as follows:

> Sometimes a book is good by reason of its written material; sometimes it acquires merit solely by the illustrations. But our two Annual Reports have, thanks to the joint efforts of yourself and your husband, reached an equally high standard of excellence in both features. Modern Colonial Reports have to be readable; you have made ours a model.

It did not take me long to find out that this letter had been inspired as well as drafted by the Under Secretary, my immediate senior in the Secretariat, who was also my infant son's godfather. No matter – it came on Government House notepaper!

My schedule of responsibilities in our office included, beside annual reports, Police, Education, Trade Unions (mostly a front for anarchistic political parties), Transport – and probably a number of others I have forgotten. The last item covered every kind of conveyance from rickshaws to aircraft. The proposed abolition of the rickshaw was one of the earliest matters to be discussed. Just after the war we had all become very conscious of the dignity of man, and it seemed wrong that one should have to earn his living by pulling along another. To propel him in a

Colonial Postscript

bicycle sidecar was somehow different, and this system of transport was allowed to continue. I think we thought up this piece of social legislation for ourselves, but there were also many conventions which the International Labour Office had drafted, with a view to preventing the exploitation of workers, which we were invited to adopt. At the opposite end of the scale was the question of airport development. The pre-war aerodrome at Kallang was too small for the new aircraft and, besides, when taking off they ran the risk of grazing the spire of St Andrew's cathedral. Volumes were written about where a new international airport should be situated, and how it was to be paid for. It was not the job of the secretariat staff to contribute to this discussion, but rather to make sure that eveyone who should be was consulted, and then to coordinate and attempt some conclusions from what they had all said. Now I began to have some sympathy with the civil servant from the Treasury I had met in Ceylon who would not get out of the car to see with his own eyes the site of the proposed transit camp. Unlike him, I paid several visits to the favoured location at Changi, putting myself in the position of a traveller arriving in Singapore for the first time, and thinking what a good impression of it he would receive by landing there. And there was already a runway there, built by the Japanese. But the engineers would have none of this; the runway had been built across a swamp, they said, and the site was totally unsuitable. They had their way, and the airport was built nearer the centre of the island, on the edge of the built-up area of the city. Only a few years later this too was abandoned, and Changi was chosen for the new international airport, which has not, so far as I know, subsided into the swamp. So much for expert opinion!

In the three years following the liberation of Singapore the colony had, thanks mainly to the enterprise of its inhabitants aided, I like to think, by tolerant and sensible government policies, largely overcome the three problems left by the Japanese occupation, listed in the 1946 annual report as 'the restoration of law and order, the provision of food and the elimination of the causes of social unrest'. Much of its former

Singapore continued, 1946–8

prosperity had returned to it and the general feeling was one of optimism. But all this brought little relaxation to pen-pushers like myself in the Secretariat. At about noon on Saturday mornings, a pile of telegrams would arrive from the Colonial Office, containing the text of Parliamentary Questions about Singapore which the Secretary of State had to answer the following week. Quick telephone calls had to be made all round the island to obtain the comments of the officials concerned before they all disappeared in search of beers or gins and bitters, while we had to stay on in the office well into the afternoon working out the answers. After a year of this I had made another attempt to get away but by that time the Colonial Secretary had made up his mind to keep the team he had got around him and he refused to consider a transfer. Being a countryman at heart and something of a Malay scholar too he may have had a bit of a conscience about keeping me in the city for so long, and when at last I said goodbye before going on leave he presented me with his old and treasured Malay dictionary, newly rebound and inscribed with the words 'From Patrick A. B. McKerron, Jasin 1922, to John Morley, Singapore 1948'. Jasin was the district near Malacca where he had begun his own career, and he would have liked me to follow him there. He was also my son's other godfather, and Lady McKerron a close family friend, until she died many years later.

XIV
Malaya – Ipoh and Kuala Lumpur, 1949–51

My leave fell due towards the end of the year. Having by now a family of three young children we decided against going home to England in winter time and instead booked passages to Western Australia, taking with us Nancy Chan, daughter of the Singapore postmaster, to help look after them. Regrettably, her adventures there cannot form part of a colonial memoir!

There had been a rumour that my next posting would be to Trenganu. This is a state – I visited it once – on the northeast coast of Malaya where lovely palms bend over coral beaches, the Malays live in stilted kampongs, and the way of life hasn't changed very much during the generations it has been known to the outside world. Instead of which, I learnt that I was to be sent to Ipoh, a town like Singapore, more Chinese than Malay, a centre of the tin mining industry and centre too for the bandit activity which had broken out while we were away. Even trains were sometimes ambushed and, on boarding the night mail in Singapore we were both alarmed and amused to read a notice saying that, if they should hear firing 'passengers are requested to lay [sic] on the floor'. Arriving at Ipoh we put up at first in a hotel, but moved soon into a lovely house, only a short walk across the racecourse from the office of the British Adviser, whose assistant I was to be. But the Adviser liked to keep everything under his own control, and did not really want any assistance. For the first time in my life, almost, I had too little to do.

The state of Perak, whose Sultan we were supposed to be

Malaya – Ipoh and Kuala Lumpur, 1949–51

advising, was infested not only by bandits but also by tigers, which had multiplied during the Japanese occupation, and become a nuisance to the inhabitants. So various tiger hunts were organized, in some of which I found myself taking part. They had little in common with the events one has read about in India. Here the hunt consisted simply of hunters armed with rifles or shotguns standing with their backs to one another in a clearing, while beaters drove any game in their direction through the jungle. No tigers appeared when I was present but, after only one experience of this 'sport' I took out a supplementary life insurance.

With time on my hands, I took up a subject which had interested me in Singapore and even earlier, the role of the Arabs in the Far Eastern trade. A paper I gave on the subject to the local Rotarians which was reported in the *Malaya Tribune* was followed by one on the same theme by the Chinese consul, and soon others joined in, among them Che Albakri, the influential State Secretary, who produced details of his own Arab ancestry. This was not the first time I had come across the spellbinding power of genealogy; in Africa it had been a common experience to meet illiterate nomads who could, and if given any encouragement would, recite without hesitation the names and personal particulars of ancestors going back many generations. Another person keenly interested was the newly-appointed High Commissioner, Sir Henry Gurney. He was, like myself, an 'African', having come from Kenya, where Arabs had traded and colonized for centuries before the arrival of Western influences, just as they had done in Malaya. When he came to Ipoh for an investiture we had a long talk about them. Perhaps it was this conversation that led to my being transferred, very soon afterwards, to the Secretariat in Kuala Lumpur.

The new High Commissioner of the Federation had taken over at a difficult moment when not only was the authority of the government being challenged by Communist forces able to rely on the sympathy, if not the active support, of one part of the population, the Chinese, but the other part of the population, the Malays, had had their confidence badly shaken by the attempt, ultimately unsuccessful, of his predecessor, working on a plan conceived in Whitehall, to combine all the juridically independent states of the peninsula into a Malayan Union. Sir Henry believed that one of the ways of diverting attention from this political miscalculation and recreating confidence would be to draw up a social and economic development plan for the country's future. This would also fit in well with thinking at the Colonial Office which, at that time, was decidedly planning-conscious. So much can be read between the lines of his preface to a yellow-bound volume *Draft Development Plan of the Federation of Malaya*, 'Paper to be laid before the Federal Legislative Council by command of His Excellency the High Commissioner'. The preparation of this Plan and indeed the writing of a great part of it was the work I had been called down to do, and, while it was disappointing not to be going out to a district, this was an interesting and seemingly worthwhile task. I was fortunately unaware, when engaged on it, that plans of this sort very often get overtaken by events almost as soon as they are written – as happened on this occasion too, when the outbreak of the Korean War sent prices rocketing. For all that, it helped the High Commissioner achieve his purpose and did, in many cases, provide a benchmark against which further progress could be judged.

After the main work in connection with the plan was finished I settled down into the Economic Secretariat which, as in Singapore, was housed in a separate building from the main office. The separation was necessary because of insufficient space, though I am sure there was also a lurking feeling that economic matters were slightly irrelevant to the main business of running a country. We on the opposite side of the street naturally took the opposite view, pointing out that the whole apparatus of government could collapse like a pricked balloon if it were deprived of the support of the two great industries of tin and rubber, through the price of either falling to a low level over a long period. The Economic Secretary, who was an old Malayan Civil Service hand, had charge of the tin industry while I, his Deputy, looked after rubber; then when he went on leave

Malaya – Ipoh and Kuala Lumpur, 1949–51

prior to retirement I for a time stepped into his shoes and was sworn in as a member of the Federation's Executive and Legislative Councils, but I was not considered senior enough to hold that position permanently. The High Commissioner, who returned from leave about this time, had been in touch with the Colonial Office about a substantive holder of the post, and had been informed by them that a man called Spencer was available for the appointment. Concluding that this was a fellow officer he had known in East Africa, he sent a telegram confirming that this proposal was acceptable.

When the new Economic Secretary arrived, he turned out to be a different Spencer altogether. Moreover, instead of being one who had picked up the techniques as he went along, in the time-honoured Colonial Service tradition, he had been professionally trained at the London School of Economics and had all the self-confidence that went with it. Malaya reeled under the shock, Sir Henry preserved a discreet silence, while I began for the first time to learn about such things as gross national products and marginal rates of return. Oscar Spencer had a clear idea of where he wanted to go and soon ended our organizational isolation – though physically we remained apart – by pushing through a plan to rename the Financial Secretary's Office the Treasury, and our own office the Economic branch of it. This move seemed to clear the way for his own promotion to Financial Secretary in due course, though that part of the plan never materialized.

All this time my family was growing up. Before the war it had been the rule not to keep European children in the tropics past the age of five. Our elder daughter at the age of seven was not doing well in the sticky heat of the Malayan plains. Luckily a school had reopened at the hill station of Cameron Highlands and thither she was sent, the pupils being escorted back and forth at the beginning and end of term by a detachment of troops, in case of possible ambush by the bandits. (It was on the road to the other hill station of Fraser's Hill that Sir Henry Gurney, who was a friend as well as a leader of his staff in Malaya, was ambushed and killed by the Communists a year or

Colonial Postscript

two later.) At the end of her first term there our pallid daughter came back looking the picture of health and it was this I suppose which made me realize that the days of our united family home were already numbered. So often in life one embarks on a course of action which has predictable but uncomfortable consequences, and one closes one's eyes to this future prospect, hoping that by so doing one will cause it to pass away! I had given my heart to the Colonial Service, enjoyed myself immensely working in it and had some modest successes. Now for the first time I faced the harsh fact that, if I stayed on in the service, my family would be permanently divided.

But what was the alternative? And, if I left the service, how could I do so without forfeiting whatever pension rights had been earned? Normally, these would be lost by premature retirement, but there was one set of circumstances where this rule did not apply, if the territory in which one was serving ceased to be a colony, set up its own establishment and gave its civil servants the option of staying on or retiring and taking their pension rights with them. Now about this time it was announced that the Gold Coast in West Africa was to be granted independence, the first British colony to travel along this road, and to that colony accordingly I sought and obtained a transfer. The actual date of independence had not been announced, and in the event the Gold Coast achieved it not long in advance of Malaya, but no one could have foreseen this at the time. A further thought in our minds was that, as West Africa was so much nearer home than the Far East, the inevitable separations still to come could be more easily and more cheaply surmounted. And finally the post for which I had applied sounded unusually interesting and would mean a big advance in salary – but more about that in the next chapter. No reply to my application had been received when we packed our belongings for the umpteenth time before flying back to England on leave, though as we waved goodbye I felt fairly sure that we would not be returning to Malaya, and that I had heard the last of tin and rubber. But the latter turned out to be not quite correct.

For, after I had been home for only a short while, the Foreign

Malaya – Ipoh and Kuala Lumpur, 1949–51

Office rang up one day to say that one of the six lecture tours to the United States they sponsored every year was in danger of falling through on account of the illness of the lecturer, and they would like me to go in his place. I think they had cleared with the Colonial Office that my leave could be extended for this purpose, as the tour would take eight weeks. The other speaker would have lectured on the British banking system; I was to do so on the British in Malaya. The switch of subjects had been made at such short notice that, I found, a number of audiences were not advised about it. They did not seem to mind. Memories of the war in Europe were still green in the American mind, and they were keen to show hospitality to a British visitor, whatever his background. Indeed, an English voice seemed to mesmerize them, no matter what it said. It was a tough schedule, with speaking engagements two or three times a day, from the eastern states to San Diego in southern California – where I found Bill Miller, cultivating his avocado orchard, who greeted me like a visitor from another planet. With the same twinkle in his eye as of old in Massawa, he informed me that he had promoted himself from Colonel to General, the higher rank going down better in the local community! But let not that be held against the memory of an officer under whom I was proud to have served.

A principal object of my mission, according to the briefing I had been given, was to defend British government policy in allowing exports of Malayan rubber to Communist China, about which the American press had been making a great fuss. I went prepared to do so, but found that attention had shifted to other issues by the time I got there. My report on the trip included the remark that

> ...of all the countries along the Pacific seaboard the two about which America knows least are Malaya and Indo-China; they feel they have no part to play in the economic development of these countries ... This attitude is quite unjustifiable considering the major economic and strategic interests America has in S.E. Asia

Colonial Postscript

A prophetic comment, in the light of subsequent U.S. involvement in Vietnam.

In retrospect I feel somewhat ashamed to have spent two years in Malaya's capital city, Kuala Lumpur, and to have made so few friends among the Malayan people. The nature of my job, family commitments and the restriction on movement in the country resulting from the emergency contributed to this sorry state of affairs, but even so ... From my superficial contacts I came away with an impression of gentleness of character, unwillingness to take anything to extremes, but at the same time considerable determination. A people, some thought, who might have difficulty in standing up to the destructive forces of Western materialism once the supporting props were removed. Yet few of the new nation-states have conducted themselves since independence with as balanced a judgment, as sound a sense of practical possibilities. It seems that the Malay personal philosophy was a lot tougher than was generally realized.

XV
Gold Coast, 1952–6

Accra, the capital of Ghana, Gold Coast as it then was, is an open roadstead where the West African surf pounds incessantly below those former citadels of the slave trade, Christianborg Castle and James Fort, the one become Government House of the colony, the other converted into a prison. Here Kwame Nkrumah had been detained, with some of his lieutenants, after the riots of 1950, but he was released when his party, the Convention People's Party (C.P.P.), won a sweeping victory at the first general election, and invited by the governor, Sir Charles Arden-Clarke, to form a government. On arrival I reported to Sir Charles, who spelt out the situation in a few well-chosen words. 'In your former posts,' he said 'you have been concerned with building things up. Here you may find that they are running down. It will be your task to ensure that they do not run down too rapidly.' By then it was twelve months after the C.P.P.'s government had taken office, and things did not appear to be running below the level of efficiency that one might expect. The new administration – which was not entirely African or entirely elected, since it included an official Chief Secretary, Financial Secretary and Attorney General, who were Europeans – was on its best behaviour, with one eye on the British Government, the other on the less predictable United Nations, under whom the United Kingdom held a sizeable part of the territory (a slice of the former German territory of Togoland) in trust, and whose agreement would be necessary before the trust could be terminated and the province transferred. The new African ministers were helped in their unfamiliar

Colonial Postscript

task by the buoyant state of the economy, which as often happens was not in any way due to the policies of the government in power, but was as always attributed to them. They were also helped by the collaboration of the civil service. When one is struggling for independence, it is hard to believe that those from whom the power is to pass are genuinely willing to surrender it. It was Arden-Clarke's achievement to have been able to persuade Nkrumah that this really was so, and although the C.P.P. continued as before to inveigh against imperialism, this was out of habit rather than from any genuine conviction.

Outside the main framework of Government ministries but of great importance to the economy and hitherto under their close control were two Marketing Boards, one for cocoa and the other for the remaining exportable Agricultural Produce, and two Development Corporations, one Industrial and the other Agricultural. All four organizations were now to be released from day-to-day official direction, so that greater powers and responsibilities could be exercised by members of their Boards, in future to be composed entirely of Africans. However it was felt that some supervision would still be required in the early stages, and the goverment decided that this called for a new appointment. As a result there appeared in 1951 in *The Economist*, a magazine which was required reading in Oscar Spencer's office, an advertisement for the post of 'Special Commissioner, Development Corporations and Marketing Boards', in the Gold Coast. The post was pensionable, and therefore part of the civil service, but it was evidently not intended for existing members. For one thing, posts in the normal establishment would not be advertised, but were filled by selection, for another, the salary offered was such as might be expected to attract an outsider. When it was given to an insider, this caused some initial trouble in the Gold Coast, where posts in the civil service were graded in the staff list, and the relative seniority of their holders thus established, by the amount of salary attached to them. The older hands would not have objected to a complete stranger coming in at this level, but with someone from their own service doing so they feared there might

Gold Coast, 1952–6

be competition for promotion. The trouble was short-lived; as the pace of constitutional development quickened over the next few years the expatriate civil service had more serious problems to think about than seniority or precedence.

My recollections of the Elder Dempster line mailboats which plied between Liverpool and the West African ports were vivid ones. These ships were an extension of the West African scene, just as the P&O steamers had been of the Far East. Before the war the passenger list was predominantly male, and the seasoned coasters were, even before the ship had cast off from its downriver berth, settled in front of gins and bitters in the smokingroom chairs they would hardly vacate for the rest of the voyage. By 1952 the men were in a minority. The coasters had taken to travelling by air, leaving the ship to tourists making the round trip, to wives going out to join their husbands and – greatest innovation of all – to hordes of young children. Only a few officials, miners, traders or missionaries still made the sea trip either for sentimental reasons or because, like me, they had old-fashioned ideas about travelling with baggage or the cars they bought on leave from which they did not want to get separated. But while the style of the journey had changed, the town of Accra, at the other end of it, still looked the old-style colonial capital, with its ever-open Syrian and Indian owned stores, whose long counters gave onto street sidewalks flanked by deep stormwater drains, with its colourful, multi-coloured population, with its miniature cathedral, with a bank or two built in the days when bank managers lived over the shop, and with the inevitable European club and golf course. Only on the outskirts of the town, tall blocks of flats were rising while, in the centre, holes in the ground marked the site of new offices. Government had been expanding in a hurry, and round the old Secretariat with its spacious rooms and creaking floors sprawled a number of semi-permanent buildings, put up at short notice to accommodate the new Ministries. In one of these I was given a temporary home, in the furthest office of the outermost block, facing a no-man's land of long grass and sandy waste where the caretaker, a Hausa man from the north, grew a few plants of straggling cassava and kept some hungry chickens. These wandered in and out in search of crumbs from the biscuits which my secretary, who was pregnant, kept in her drawer and nibbled surreptitiously. I was glad to find that, in the modern Accra, the spirit of Africa as I had known it was still very much alive.

The Gold Coast Cocoa Marketing Board was much the most important of the four organizations which were to be my concern during the next four years. Modelled on the British marketing boards it differed from them in the important respect that its producer members were appointed, instead of being elected, which of course meant that to a man they were not merely loyal but militant followers of the C.P.P. The Board operated by declaring a price to farmers at the beginning of the season for all the cocoa in the Gold Coast, of which it was the sole buyer, keeping for itself the difference between that and the world price, at which it sold. It performed this buying operation through licensed agents, which were mostly the big importing firms, though the co-operatives too had a fair share of the business. As a result of good luck, deliberate intention and extreme caution – particularly the last – the Board had by the mid-fifties accumulated about £80 million in reserves, more than the value of the annual crop, more indeed than the reserves of the Government itself. The greater part of them was held in practically liquid form in British Government securities, earning an interest of 3 per cent. The main justification for this policy, as thought out afterwards, was that it was prudent to keep down the price to the farmer during the years following the war, when both capital and consumer goods were in short supply, and a higher price would merely have led to intense inflation and left no one better off. This was probably so, but it might have been better if Government itself could have become the owner of these vast balances. As things were they were left with the Board, and the new men in power there, persons of little education or background (as was the case with C.P.P. supporters generally) found themselves in possession of a treasure chest which it needed little skill to open. And, when they had done so,

Gold Coast, 1952–6

what was to prevent them helping themselves? Nothing, except the baleful gaze of their expatriate Managing Director, me!

And so the next four years turned out to be a battle of wits, mostly good-humoured but at times deadly serious, between myself, whose aim was to ensure that any expenditure of the Board's income or accumulated funds was only for purposes authorized by the Cocoa Marketing Board Ordinance, and my African colleagues on the Board, who had quite other purposes in view. Not only private purposes, it must be added, though these were certainly not overlooked; the Convention People's Party was in great, even desperate need of funds, and looked to its representatives on the Cocoa Marketing Board to obtain them. It was this interplay of interests which made the situation so specially difficult because in the last resort the only appeal against what seemed to be a corrupt decision on the part of the Board lay to the Minister, who in his private capacity was already aware of the plan to 'milk' the Board of some of its money. Officially, all the same, he might feel compelled to take my side, once the full nature of the plan and its implications had been exposed. So this was a remedy which could be applied in a clear-cut case, provided one did not use it too often.

It was best to avoid an outright confrontation, in order that the Board, with all its imperfections, might be made to work in the way that had been intended. It had fortunately been established in the early days that the Managing Director should arrange the agenda, and be responsible for producing the minutes of meetings. Relying on the fact that the Board members would argue all matters, great or small, with equal intensity, it was possible to arrange for the more important of them to be placed well down the list, so that the members were beginning to tire, and to crave for their lunch, by the time we reached that point. They would then deal with these matters in a hurry, and be more than usually confused as to what they had agreed – if they had agreed anything at all. There is a rhyme which sums up the situation very aptly:

And so, when the great ones retire to their dinner,
The secretary stays, getting thinner and thinner,

Colonial Postscript

Racking his brains, as he strives to report
What he thinks they will think that they ought to have thought.

My conclusion, when writing the minutes, would often be that they had not taken the final decision they thought they had, and the matter would be so recorded. During the following month, before the next meeting took place, it would often be possible to have a word with the Chairman, or the individual members, to suggest a compromise which would be more within the spirit of the Ordinance. Even when a new secretary (again a C.P.P. member) was appointed, these tactics could still be followed, since he was barely literate and the minutes he produced always had to be rewritten before they made any sense. In doing so, they could be rephrased so as to bring out the more desirable aspects. Sometimes these ploys were effective, sometimes not, and in the end the battle would have to be fought out at Board meetings, where I claimed the right to speak last, before the summing up of the Chairman. It was sometimes very difficult to know just what line to take, since projects would be put forward in which personal, party and national interests were nicely intermingled; it was impossible to resist them on the first of these grounds without appearing to be obstructive as regards the last. In any case one would soon have lost any sort of control over the situation by merely saying 'No', whenever there was any doubt about the matter. Equally it would have been fatal to say 'Yes', in order to preserve good relations, since were any scandal to ensue, as one day it surely would, responsibility for the decision would certainly, and to some extent justifiably, be placed on the Managing Director. I had seen this happen to one of the European departmental heads, who had possibly not resisted strongly enough decisions that he must have known to be wrong, for which he had been made the scapegoat at an official enquiry, though not himself responsible for them.

One of the problems was how to hold the situation during periods when I was on leave, which I tried to arrange so as to miss as few Board meetings as possible, though I always found that one or two decisions had been taken which I could not go

Gold Coast, 1952-6

along with, and in such cases I had to make it clear that I would have voted against them if I had been present to do so. It was a constantly exposed and isolated position to be in, though not so unpleasant as it may sound. A redeeming feature of even the worst of these disputes was the lively sense of humour that most Africans possess; there were times when I felt that even the most intransigent would have been disappointed if I had not opposed them! There were also other currents of feeling. Some, who voted with the majority but against their own consciences, must have been secretly glad that their view was not allowed to prevail. After leaving the country I received a letter from the General Manager of the Board who, because he was an African and an employee, was subject to pressures ten times stronger than those which an expatriate ever experienced. 'I myself,' he wrote, 'am always sustained and inspired by the very high standards which you laid down and followed whilst in the country.' Despite some sharp differences of opinion on occasions I had a happy relationship with two of the three Africans who were Chairmen of the Cocoa Marketing Board during my time (the third was a boorish ruffian with whom there could be no common ground). Both of them saw the precipices looming in front of them and, while the mob howled behind, were glad to have a co-driver who insisted on applying the brakes.

For reasons to be explained later, I made extensive notes of the major issues on which the Board and then the Government had been warned about irregularities which nevertheless were allowed to continue. A case in point was the appointment by the Board (while I was on leave) of a 'field inspectorate', nominally to assist the police and customs service with the prevention of smuggling. In practice this force of several hundred strong existed for no other purpose than that of providing 'jobs for the boys', relatives of Board members or supporters of the party who had to be rewarded. But this was a trifle compared with the Cocoa Purchasing Company (C.P.C.), which succeeded in getting through £2 million in a couple of years. Only a small part of this was spent in the legitimate business of buying cocoa, the rest went in purchasing the goodwill of farmers in anticipation of the coming election or in lining the pockets of C.P.P. leaders. Naturally the opposition party complained bitterly about this, though there was more of envy than moral disapproval in their protests; if they had been in power they would have done exactly the same themselves. The formation of the C.P.C. – the near identity of its initials with C.P.P. was a gift to the leader writers – was within the powers of the Marketing Board and proved a most successsful method of diverting public funds into the party's coffers without actually contravening the law. As an original signatory to its Articles of Association I was entitled to attend its general meetings, at which I would ask for details of expenditure, but these of course were never supplied. From time to time I used to report what was going on to the Governor, who made sympathetic noises but left me to fight my own battles. He had the delicate task of steering the country towards independence and the last thing he wanted was that the already tortuous path of negotiations should be confused by this outside issue. Sometimes there seemed little point in continuing to plug one hole after another knowing full well that, the moment the country became theirs, many of our ideas about what constituted good administration would be jettisoned.

The Cocoa Marketing Board was owner of another subsidiary company, situated in London. There, from a small office in Buckingham Gate, Sir Eric Tansley sold over the telephone about two-thirds of the world's cocoa (for he handled the produce of Nigeria and Sierra Leone as well as ours) and a fair proportion of the world tonnage of palm oil and palm kernels from West Africa. He did his job nonchalantly, effectively and extremely cheaply, but it was not a system that could be expected to last after independence arrived. It would have been best to prepare for that time, and substitute an alternative, such as an auction in Accra, which would have been less efficient but also less open to abuse than one where millions of pounds were channeled through a single outlet. I had some ideas on the subject, but was unable to obtain any support for them.

Once or twice a year a party went from the Board to visit its

Gold Coast, 1952–6

UK subsidiary and several times I went with them. It was quite a responsibility at first, as several of my colleagues had never travelled before and were totally ignorant of the ways of the world outside the Gold Coast. On one famous occasion just as we were approaching the customs barrier at Heathrow airport one of the Africans whispered to me, 'What shall I do with my trinkets?' In a few hurried words he explained to me that he was carrying in his bag his entire stock of gold ornaments which, because there was no one he trusted at home, he had brought with him in his suitcase. These ornaments he now transferred to the pockets of his overcoat before he approached the customs officers, who chalked his bag and let him through. All would have been well if we had walked down the stairs instead of getting onto the moving staircase. My friend got onto this but he could not manage the getting off, and in the next moment he was lying spread-eagled on the floor, gold bangles flying in all directions.

On another occasion we all went in a hired car to visit the Bournville works near Birmingham, Cadbury & Fry being one of our most important customers. The Africans found this and the sightseeing very exhausting; they made the most cursory inspection of Shakespeare's birthplace and were totally uninterested in the Oxford colleges. On our way back to London we passed through a small village in the Chilterns where a travelling fair had been set up. The car was halted immediately, the Africans were out of the car like lightning, and spent the next hour happily at the sideshows and on the merry-go-round. How much would one of these cost, they wanted to know, thinking how well it would go down in the Gold Coast and, no doubt, that the Cocoa Marketing Board could find some means of paying for it.

Because of the immense importance of the cocoa crop to the country, all issues connected with the Cocoa Marketing Board were political issues. Moreover the selling price fluctuated wildly and in a year like 1954, when this reached £500 per ton (while the farmer continued to receive less than £140 per ton) there was a lot of money to be made out of it. In the case of one of

Colonial Postscript

my other statutory bodies, the Agricultural Produce Marketing Board, these factors were absent, and we were able to do a useful job of marketing the relatively small quantities of palm kernels, copra, coffee and shea nuts without too much political interference. Its chairman was a nice young man, later to become a Ghanaian ambassador, who created no problems, apart from putting the office telephonist in the family way, while its general manager and secretary, also young and enthusiastic, put heart and soul into the business. The handling of these minor crops was in many ways a most interesting job. Coffee was mostly produced up on the Togoland border. When the world market price rose substantially above ours in the course of the season, Gold Coast coffee all disappeared over the border into French Dahomey. If on the other hand ours was a better price, the Gold Coast crop always turned out to have been exceptionally heavy! Artificial market prices were part of the Marketing Board system; they worked where cocoa was concerned only because the crop was too heavy to be easily transportable in head-loads over the border, but coffee did not suffer from this disadvantage. (Nor did diamonds, on which I was called in to advise the Sierra Leone government some years later; the only way to prevent smuggling, I recommended, was to establish a fair market price within the national frontiers.) The shea nuts we sold were harvested from trees growing wild in the Northern Territories, which had practically no other export crop. Unfortunately very few manufactuers had developed a use for the oil extracted from them, while another difficulty was that even in that day and age the hunters and farmers in the area where they grew had not reached the stage of a cash economy; they had better things to do with their time than spend it earning money.

Accra lies in the earthquake belt, and most of the architects working there had taken the precaution of using two or three times the normal quantity of cement and steel in constructing their buildings, which often looked lumpy and ponderous in consequence. Latterly however a younger generation of men had appeared, working with reinforced concrete to produce open and graceful structures, one of the most elegant of which was a

Gold Coast, 1952–6

new building commissioned by the Industrial Development Corporatiion, to which I removed my office as soon as it was complete. This was a long way from the Secretariat and close to the business centre of downtown Accra. Along the High Street on which it abutted flowed a varied stream of traffic – food and cloth sellers swathed in rainbow colours carrying their wares on their heads, Northern Territories oxen in the final stages of decrepitude padding the last few yards to the slaughterhouse, lorries brightly painted with biblical texts, 'The Lord is my Shepherd' or political slogans, 'Forward ever Backward never' (the watchword of the C.P.P.), pi-dogs, prostitutes and policemen. But the most typical and telling sight occurred in the evening, when this traffic though still active had died down somewhat. After dark, under each street lamp along the kerb, sat two young men, back to back against the lamp-post, studying one or other of the much advertised correspondence courses which were the poor and usually quite futile substitute for the secondary education which they had been unable to obtain. Knowledge was power. What else enabled Europeans to ride in smart cars and give orders to their inferiors, if not their educational advantage? Had they not often heard in the past that this job or that job could only be held by a European because there was as yet no African trained for it? Now that an African-educated elite was beginning to emerge it was being said that other qualifications were necessary, such as experience. But the young men did not believe this. Education was the key that would open all doors. Best to get one of the Cocoa Marketing Board scholarships to study in Europe. But these were few and to get one of them it was necessary to know the right people. An alternative was to get admission to one of the new schools being opened up and down the country, far in advance of qualified teachers to staff them. For most it was a correspondence course, and a lamp in the street to study under.

There was not only a burning desire for education but a feeling of overwhelming urgency to acquire it. In 1954 new elections were scheduled. These would introduce a revised constitution in which the remaining ex officio posts would

Colonial Postscript

disappear, the Cabinet enjoy full responsibility, and the reserve powers of the Governor be practically extinguished. Then, it was assumed, though incorrectly as it turned out, the last obstacle to independence would be removed, and the way be open for a complete Africanization of all the posts until then held by expatriates, in government, commerce, or the mines. Not that there was animosity towards the Europeans, although obviously there were differences in the way they had, and Africans would run the country, but it was natural to expect their early replacement and, in the meantime, the Rapid Results College could help prepare the way.

By 1954 the political scene had changed a good deal from what it had been three years earlier, at the time of the first election. It had become clear that a party based on the support of the masses was not popular with the intelligentsia of the colony and that it was suspect also to the chiefs, whose influence was powerful in Ashanti and the Northern Territories. Secondly, the new found nationalism had not replaced the older tribalism and, in the opinion of many, too large a share of the posts in and under the government had been given to Fantis from the Cape Coast area. So, when the 1954 election fell due, while independence was still a dominant theme it was no longer the only one. A party which wished to do well would need to have other planks to its platform and would have to canvass support from all sides. The election was likely to be the last held under a colonial form of government, and elaborate preparation was made for it, by the political parties as well as by the authorities. One of the problems so far as the latter was concerned was to ensure that no one voted twice, the method of preventing this being to dip every voter's left thumb in a long-lasting dye before he left the polling station. A separate box was also provided for each candidate, so that the voter who could not read or write could put his paper in a box marked with an elephant, palm tree or other device adopted by the party for its candidates. It was said however that ingenuity defeated all these precautions. Trusted supporters stood in the crowd offering to buy votes for their party at ten shillings a time; in order to earn this money the voter had to go through all the motions of voting except the last, when he would put the paper in his own pocket instead of in one of the boxes. At the end of the day the party agent himself went to the polling station, where he posted into the right box his own vote plus all the slips he had acquired. It would have taken him too long to insert them all one by one, so he folded them into bundles, which told the tale of what had happened when the boxes were opened for the votes to be counted. Whether this was a true story or just a piece of modern folklore I never knew; it was a tale that both parties gleefully told about their opponents.

XVI
Gold Coast Concluded, 1952–6

The ground floor of the new Industrial Development Corporation building where I had my office was given over to a showroom occupied by one of the corporation's subsidiaries which sold articles of hideous design – including the ever popular Ashanti-type stool supported on elephants – made from the rich mahoganies for which the Gold Coast was famous. Before the war the pottery, the rush mats, the wool and cotton blankets, the brass and woodwork produced in Africa south of the Sahara still preserved that unselfconscious quality of goods which are fabricated for use and only incidentally for admiration. During and after the war the growth in demand from tourists especially led to mass production of these articles by a new generation of craftsmen who were inevitably more influenced by what would sell in the airport shops than what would appeal to their own people, who in any case were ceasing to use some home-made materials and whose tastes were becoming internationalized. The Gold Coast was more fortunate than some countries in having strong local traditions – in the weaving of kenti cloth for example – which did not yield easily to innovation. The same was true in some respects of wood carving, as may be seen from the fine head and half torso of a mother and child in odum wood (perhaps by Kofi Antubam) which we bought at an exhibition got up by Dr Ampofo at Aburi. In this African and European influences have been most harmoniously brought together.

Another I.D.C. subsidiary was the Brick & Tile Company at Weija, whose clay and kiln we used for the terra cotta heads

Gold Coast Concluded, 1952–6

which Pat had begun to make, and which were splendidly illustrated in a *Corona* magazine of this period. Mostly she worked in pastel, collecting material for an exhibition sponsored by the British Council and opened by Kwame Nkrumah, who inspected the portraits and then left without uttering a single word, his customary charisma completely deserting him on this occasion. In another issue of the same magazine I described how some of these pictures had been obtained, beginning with an account of a visit to the small town of Pankese, where the I.D.C. had a sawmill and where

> the Pankesihene, or chief of the place, produced a number of gold ornamental objects from the state regalia, a coronet, a bracelet and a staff of office which, added to his own rather fine head, looked as though they would make an interesting picture. They weren't really gold, of course; even by the light of the Tilley lamp one could see the ornaments were carved out of wood and covered with gold paint, but they were very decorative, especially the coronet, where the design of yellow flowers stood out effectively against the black velvet background.
>
> The chief was pleased to be drawn but not so his elders whom he had by custom to consult the next morning. They were highly suspicious, and would not at first believe that the customary present, of schnapps and beer, had no ulterior purpose. In fact, it was perhaps an excessive fee for a single sitting, but this was the first time a Pankesihene had been asked to sit for his portrait, and there were no precedents to guide one. What was the real object, they wanted to know? A timber concession, perhaps? Then they shifted their ground and declared that, if their chief were to be painted, all of them should be. This was not so unreasonable as it seemed, for the interpreter had been making free use of the word 'photo', and when the difference between a camera and a sketch book was demonstrated they did not press the point. Instead they said they would all stay and watch. The trials of being a court painter! By this time the official council had swollen to a

Colonial Postscript

sizeable throng, and the thesis that village government in the Gold Coast is highly democratic and representative of the popular will was becoming a self-evident fact . . .

A much remarked fact about the Gold Coast is the extent to which its peoples have become mixed up. This applies not merely to the towns but to many rural areas also, where large numbers of the population may be found to have migrated either temporarily or permanently from other regions. At a village well off the main routes in the Central Province the two or three people who were called in as possible models had all come from homes in distant French Togoland. A lakeside village in Ashanti, only a few miles away from the reputed birthplace of the Ashanti nation, was swarming with Fantis – all the Ashanti models were picked up in other parts of the country. The vegetable gardens on the outskirts of Accra, a favourite source of supply for sitters, seemed to be exclusively controlled by Busangas, who had come all the way on foot from Haute Volta. Most of the office watchmen were Moshis or Fulani . . . It was only to be expected that the camp followers of expatriates in the cantonment area should be expatriates themselves – Ijaws from the Niger delta were particularly in evidence – but one was hardly prepared for the diversity of countries from which they had come. Nor, when it came to drawing them, was one prepared for the extreme variety of appearance they presented, with features which, on analysis, often differed little from those to be found in Europe. It was colour alone which distinguished them.

Most numerous of all it seemed – possibly because they could be more easily identified – were the people from the Northern Territories and from French territory beyond. 'Pure complete bushmen,' an Ijaw sitter once named them, taking his own rather superficial view of what constituted civilization. One of these, a Buzu from beyond Gao on the Niger bend, was a specially favourite model, who sat at least half a dozen times. He was a fine man in many ways; he had perfectly formed features and a strong and agile body. When talking, which he loved to do, his eyes flashed, his limbs were

Gold Coast Concluded, 1952–6

in constant movement, and his personality more than filled the small room where he sat. He was night watchman on the top of Legon, the hill which crowns the new university site and commands wide views of the sea and the escarpment to the north of the Accra plain. He had led an adventurous life, having done the journey overland to Tripoli on the Mediterranean coast several times, and all but died of thirst on one occasion. It seemed strange that so active and still young a man should be content with such a job but the pay was good and there were moments of excitement when pilferers came by night to see what they could find – but never more than once, one imagined, if they had experience of the long bayonet shaped sword which he kept sharpened to a fine point for such occasions.

One part of the Industrial Development Corporation's job was to develop industry in the Gold Coast; the other was the responsibility for promoting Africans in business. This second objective encountered many difficulties. It had been the women who traditionally engaged in commerce, while the men occupied themselves with agriculture or other pursuits. Industry was something new; it was for men, but they approached it from an uncommercial standpoint. Probably the people helped by the I.D.C. were wrongly selected, because of their political or family influence, but even so its record of failure with its loan scheme was abysmal. The emergent industrialist had no sooner got his head above water than he found himself swamped by a flood of social obligations towards relatives, so that he was never able to make a good start. Indeed much of the migration to different parts of Africa which I mentioned in my *Corona* article may have been due to the desire to shake clear of these oppressive family responsibilities. Another handicap to our work was the general unfamiliarity with tools and machinery, the result of years of misplaced emphasis on literary education. Machines were ordered from showrooms or glossy catalogues, developed some simple fault and thereafter lay idle because the owner had no idea how to service or maintain them.

Colonial Postscript

My chairman in the Industrial Development Corporation, and later in the Agricultural Development Corporation as well, naturally had to be a member of the Convention People's Party. Although he had not been active in its early campaigning he carried weight in the party's councils partly by reason of his age, which was somewhat above that of most of the leaders, and also because of his influence with the Ga people, the tribe who lived in and around Accra, which was Nkrumah's own constituency. Willie Halm was shrewd enough to see that, given the political and social conditions in which it had to work, there was little a body like the I.D.C. could do successfully to promote industry in the Gold Coast by means of small loans to individuals, and that it would win nothing but disrepute by making and failing in such an attempt. Without making an issue of the matter he quietly cut down the number of these loans to the minimum that he thought his political masters would tolerate and concentrated his interest on the larger ventures which could afford expatriate management for a period while Africans were in training. With this in view we started a number of businesses in addition to those mentioned, such as an oil mill, a bakery, a laundry, a tyre servicing company, a cigar factory, a nail factory, a hotel and many others. I got to know Halm quite well and for a long while enjoyed his full confidence. One of the reasons for this may have been my insistence that the British accountant we had caught fiddling the books should be handed over to the police and dealt with like any other offender – no doubt he had expected me to invoke some sort of tribal protection system on his behalf!

When Halm took over chairmanship of the Agricultural Development Corporation we did a lot of travelling together, since one of its subsidiaries, the Gonja Development Corporation, was at the back end of the Northern Territories. On the journey there we had to drive for hours along laterite roads through interminable bush, stopping only for the occasional ferry, never needing to alter pace or take heed of the monotonous earthy amber and dull green hemming us in on all sides except for the one slit on the skyline where the road reached the

Gold Coast Concluded, 1952–6

peak of its present gradient and began its long descent on the other side. Dust seeped into the car every time it jolted over a bump or hollow, turning my white face brown and Halm's brown face dark orange. He could never stay awake in a car for more than a few minutes, and was soon slumped asleep in his own corner or, inconveniently, against my shoulder. He felt himself as much a stranger in this bush country as I did – probably more so – and laughed inordinately at my 'miles and miles of Africa' story; we were two expatriates enjoying a joke about a foreign country together. He was always mindful of these shared experiences and later, on my fall from grace, he did his best to warn me and, I believe, to intervene on my behalf.

The Agricultural Development Corporation had a different range of problems. A principal object was to promote crops which would lessen the country's dependence on cocoa. There were possibilities for rubber, oilpalm, cotton and other crops, but the basic information needed to make a start was lacking, since no general soil survey existed, and there was almost no meteorological data. The university Department of Agriculture, whose Professor was a personal friend, was interested and anxious to help, but its own experiments on soil fertility had only just begun and it would be in no position to give advice for several years. So we started with a number of small schemes which would not lose us too much money – several acres of high-yielding tomatoes which we lost to eelworm, a plantation of pineapples all of which ripened at the same time and presented us with a marketing problem, an oil palm scheme which proved abortive at the first attempt as the co-operative on which it was to be based split up before it got under way. This kind of set-back was to be expected, but there were no obstacles except one which could not have been overcome in a year or two. The apparently insuperable difficulty was the African general manager who had been wished on us by the Agricultural Department because they had found him so useless – and in the end Willie Halm found a way round that problem too.

The Gold Coast after the 1954 elections was in an unsettled state. The National Liberation Movement, the opposition party,

Colonial Postscript

won a number of seats in Ashanti, to whose long-standing hostility to the Colony was now added the grievance of a cocoa price maintained at an artificially low level in order, it was alleged, that the Government and not the cocoa farmer should obtain most of the benefit. It was a time for statesmanship, but instead the leaders of the C.P.P. seemed to throw discretion to the winds. From the kind of appoitments that were being made and decisions that were being taken it was all too clear where their true interests lay.

Underlying the envy of the C.P.P. harboured by those who did not enjoy the fruits of office to which party members had access, and the tensions created by its policies, there was what seemed to an outside observer to be a basically quarrelsome disposition in the Gold Coast, or, as we were now learning to call them, the Ghanaian people. (Ghana had been the first of the five empires which rose in the 8th to 18th centuries in the Western Sudan, a thousand miles away from the territory which was now adopting its name.) If this judgment seems too severe then let us say that the individual never seemed to allow that his own personal ambitions might have to be limited by the larger claims of the community. Policies were subordinated to personalities and there was continuous intrigue, which led to decisions taken one day being inexplicably reversed on the next, and often changed yet again on the morrow. This made the conduct of business very difficult and created a sense of insecurity for everyone, European or African, who was working for the government. Much of the dishonesty and corruption which occurred could be attributed to this circumstance.

'Abine stated that Ekua said that Eki used her relations with Kweku to get contract through the District Commissioner with the support of the Regional Commissioner and the blessing of a Minister in Accra.' Kwame Nkrumah understood his people and in this speech reproved them for behaviour which he genuinely felt to be unbecoming. As for himself he had no need to canvass other opinions or seek support, because he was so sure of his own destiny. And that was his ultimate misfortune; while the objects of policy were still relatively straightforward this single-

Gold Coast Concluded, 1952–6

mindedness of purpose was all very well, but as soon as the problems of government began to be more complicated his lack of political skill became very apparent. Even before independence had been won for the Gold Coast, Nkrumah saw himself in the larger role of liberator of Africa; he was absorbed in this dream and incapable of grasping the necessity for patient endeavour to weld the tribal society of the country into a single nation and to build its social and economic future securely on the base that the colonial power had prepared. Even so, he towered above the other leaders of his party, most of whom were concerned with nothing except self advancement.

The post-election period was then a time for greatness, but most of the opportunities were missed. The party journal, *The Evening News,* continued to pour out a stream of vituperation against the opposition, while the indiscipline of the party leaders was followed in its lower ranks. Proposals came before the Industrial Development Corporation which it was increasingly difficult to justify from any commercial standpoint, the promoters being a new brand of expatriate businessmen who saw the chance of quick enrichment and were not backward in approaching the I.D.C. chairman with schemes for their mutual advantage. I found myself excluded from these discussions and so only able to question the policy at Board meetings, instead of having it out in private beforehand. At these meetings the way the Board would vote was a foregone conclusion, because all concerned had been squared. Such a situation could not continue, and I suggested that the time had come when the Corporation should have only a Chairman and a General Manager, dispensing with the post of Managing Director. A similar situation was developing at the same time in the other statutory bodies.

What went on in the I.D.C. boardroom was not in the public eye. On the other hand the activities of the Cocoa Purchasing Company attracted continuous attention as they were conducted mainly in those areas of the country where the opposition party was most firmly established, and they had become an open scandal. C.P.C. funds had been liberally used for buying support

Colonial Postscript

for the C.P.P. during the election and the opposition was determined to expose these malpractices now, while there was still the authority of the Secretary of State to be appealed to. The Government was in a quandary. If they resisted the demand they must inevitably raise doubts in the mind of the British Parliament as to the readiness of the Gold Coast for independence. If they acceded to it they ran a considerable risk of evidence being given which would implicate the C.P.P. In the circumstances the best course seemed to be to allow the enquiry to take place but to do everything possible in the meantime to ensure that if any awkward questions were asked there would be no one who was both able and willing to supply a truthful answer.

The only person who came near to being in this position was myself, and I had only arrived there by accident. Four years ago, when the Cocoa Purchasing Company was being set up by the Cocoa Marketing Board it had been necessary to find several signatories of its Articles of Association, and I had been one of them. In turn, the Articles declared these signatories to be shareholders of the company. In that capacity I had the right once a year to attend its general meeting and, although it was clear that my presence there was not exactly welcome, I had regularly done so. The very minimum of information was provided, but still there was an opportunity of asking questions on the accounts, or on the absence of accounts, of noting reservations made by the auditors, and of submitting reports afterwards to the Board and to the Ministry. The reports to the Board were in a sense a formality, since all its members other than myself were appointed Directors of the Cocoa Purchasing Company, from which they drew a supplementary salary and about which they knew far more than I could possibly tell them. The reports to the Ministry were another matter, and in the light of these the Government could not possibly say at the enquiry that they had not known what was going on.

Before the date of the enquiry into the C.P.C. was fixed, or it was even certain that an enquiry would take place, action was in train to abolish the post of Managing Director in the various

Gold Coast Concluded, 1952–6

Boards and Corporations of which I was a member. Legislation to this effect was to be introduced, the post of Special Commissioner would disappear from the staff list, and the date of my departure from the Gold Coast had been settled with the various Ministries concerned. Unhappily for the Government it now appeared that this date, and the date fixed for the opening of the enquiry into the affairs of the Cocoa Purchasing Company would overlap by about four weeks. It was not or did not appear possible to postpone the enquiry, and this left only one alternative. All of a sudden, out of the blue, I received a letter instructing me to go on leave not on the date originally arranged, but immediately. This set all the alarm bells ringing, for while the Government on their side might be anxious about the evidence I could give at the enquiry, I was no less concerned on mine about the possible consequences of not being there to give it. 'I have no desire to participate in the enquiry, wish to make no statement and sincerely hope that I will not be called on to give any evidence,' I replied to the Minister the day after receiving his letter.

I cannot however ignore the fact that I have been Managing Director of the parent body, the C.M.B., during the whole of the period that the subsidiary company has been in existence, or that the Committee may wish to call upon me to give evidence, or the risk that, in the course of evidence given by some other witness, allegations of negligence or worse may be made against me which I should wish to answer.

My fears were not in fact about a possibility, but a probability, for I knew that the Government would have no scruples about what they might need to do to protect themselves. I accordingly appealed against the Minister's direction and continued sitting tight after he had confirmed it, and even after the direction had been upheld by the Prime Minister. In the end the Government gave way, fearing a showdown in which they would clearly be in the wrong and which would be likely to result in awkward questions in Parliament. Instead they managed to make new

Colonial Postscript

arrangements which would postpone the opening of the enquiry until the week after the date when I must, in any case, leave the country.

This was a barren victory for me since it appeared that the Government had achieved its main purpose of carrying on the enquiry in my absence, and that my reputation was as much at risk as ever. Three weeks of idleness remained for me – since I was no longer employed in any of my former offices – which I was able to make good use of in two ways. The first was to carry out a long postponed ambition of reading *The Iliad* of which, perhaps with some premonition of the future, I had brought the text with me. The other was to compose a detailed statement, point by point, with copious references to Cocoa Marketing Board minutes (of which, most prudently, I had retained a personal copy), recording all the objections made, all the warnings given to the Board and to the Minister, all the advice unheeded. They ran to 16 pages of closely typed foolscap and they were dynamite! Just before leaving, and just before the C.P.C. enquiry was due to open, I sent copies to the Board and to the Ministry, mentioning in my covering letter with studied casualness that, for the protection of my own interests, I had instructed a firm of solicitors to act as necessary on my behalf in my absence. In fact I had briefed them carefully and had arranged that they should let it be known in the right quarters that I would return to the Gold Coast at my own expense, and apply to give evidence, if ever there were the slightest suggestion of my conduct as Managing Director of the Cocoa Marketing Board being called in question. This arrangement worked perfectly, and four months after my return to the United Kingdom I received a letter from the solicitors as follows:

> During the course of the proceedings we were unable to arrange for you to be represented, except at an exorbitant figure, but through the kind offices of various people attending the enquiry, we were able to keep track of what was said, and it is quite clear that at no time were there any adverse

Gold Coast Concluded, 1952–6

comments made in reference to your conduct. We return to you the file you left with us and a note of our charges.

And so, for the sum of £17/15/- in solictors' fees, my 20 years with the Colonial Service came to an end in rather inglorious circumstances, although there were some hidden compensations. One of these was that I was able to turn my back on these happy years and begin looking forward to a new career with fewer regrets about the past than might have been the case under more cheerful conditions. Another was to appreciate the truth, which is only to be learnt by personal experience, that it is the effort itself which is always important; whether or not this earns the results one feels it deserves is something which is often too far outside one's control to be relevant as an indication of its value.

Some few months before these events I had been driving through one of the remoter parts of the Northern Territories and had called in with a letter, or whatever it was that I had undertaken to deliver to him on my way through, for the Assistant District Commissioner in charge of a small out-station. It happened to be Empire Day, which was still a public holiday in those days, and so I looked for him first in his bungalow. Not finding him at home, I went on to his office, but that was closed. Finally I ran him to earth doing an overtime job checking the stores in the Government dispensary, an airless room slightly impregnated with the smell of a corpse which lay in the mortuary across the road. The best time to do this job, he explained, while everyone else was out of the way. In that little incident, which happened to come back to my mind at this point, I seem to find the epitome of so much that British rule stood for in Africa, including its dedication, its obsession with often trivial detail and, more than anything, its essential incongruity. Everyone was enjoying the Empire day holiday except for the empire builder and the corpse. There is something surrealistic about its presence in this story, but I have never been sure exactly what!

The staff of the four corporations provided the traditional send-off party, but it had to be a modest and even slightly secretive affair, since everyone knew about the political implications of the situation, and most of the Africans found it more prudent to stay away. Willie Halm was indeed the only one who came, risking his political future by doing so. I am glad to say that it did him no harm, for he went on to become Chairman of the Ghanaian Black Star Shipping Company and Chairman of the Ghana National Bank, though he did go to prison in the end, after the Nkrumah regime was overturned, with the rest of the party bosses, for alleged malpractices. In the end the past usually catches up with one, though it often takes a long time.